Step Six is the Step that separates the men from the boys." So declares a well loved clergyman who happens to be one of the recovering gangsters' greatest friends. He goes on to explain that any person capable of enough willingness and honesty to repeatedly try Step Six on all his faults *without any reservations whatever* has indeed come a long way spiritually, and is therefore entitled to be called a man who is sincerely trying to grow in the image and likeness of his own Creator...........................73

When, by such simple devices, we have placed

ourselves in a mood in which we can focus undisturbed on constructive imagination, we might proceed like this: Once more we read our prayer, and again try to see what its inner essence is. We'll think now about the man who first uttered the prayer. First of all, he wanted to become a "channel." Then he asked for the grace to bring love, forgiveness, harmony, truth, faith, hope, light, and joy to every human being he could

As the day goes on, we can pause where situations must be met and decisions made, and renew the simple request: "Thy will, not mine, be done." If at these points our emotional disturbance happens to be great, we will most surely keep our balance, provided we remember, and repeat to ourselves, a particular prayer or phrase that has appealed to us in our reading or meditation. Just saying it over and over will often enable us to clear a channel choked up with anger, fear, frustration, or misunderstanding, and permit us to return to our search for God's will, not our own, in the moment of stress. At these critical moments, if we remind ourselves that "it is better to comfort than to be comforted, to understand than to be understood, to love than to be loved," we will be following the intent

Updated this 08/17/2007 Gangsters Anonymous Twelve Steps and Twelve Traditions Copyright ©2002 by Gangsters All rights reserved. Gangsters Anonymous Published 2002 first Edition 2002. Printed in the United States of America Library of Congress Cataloging in Publication Data ISBN #-######-##-# (Hardcover) Catalog Item No. ISBN #-######-###-# (Paperback) Catalog Item No Library of Congress Catalog No. 02-##### is GA Fellowship-approved literature Gangsters Anonymous and the registered Trademarks of Gangsters Anonymous, Incorporated. This logo is a Registered Published 2002 by Gangsters Anonymous (G.A.) ® in these United States. Copyright © 2002 by Gangsters Anonymous (G.A.) ® Los Angeles, CA, U.S. Of A. IBEFACE Gangsters Anonymous (G.A.) ®, www.gangstersanonymous.org <http://.www.gangstersanonymousglobalservicesinc org> ® are registered trademarks of G.A.

G.A. is a fellowship of people who are serious about their work to recover life – their own, and the life of others from the suicidal mission of gang life and criminal behavior. This first edition of G.A. is the most comprehensive single volume of its kind. Origin of this book lies in the hearts of many whose recovery from crime has rewarded them with a life unimaginable. In addition, words of wisdom cames from within the many colored books of "Twelve Steps and Twelve Traditions" by Gangsters Anonymous (G.A.) Global Services, Inc. Those in recovery from gang life welcome what similarities there may be, but understand that full and complete recovery from a gangster mentality and criminal life requires the G.A. Program where recovery from gangs and crime is not all there is to recovery. With a Higher Power, we are up to the strategic task of saving life no matter the challenge. Collaborators from all over the United States shall remain anonymous since their aim is to serve gangsters in recovery, one gangster at a time without the interference of outside agitators. As gang areas are extending and knowledge of those territories expand, professionals, lay people, and ordinary citizens are often upset. Although newly established, G.A. has many years of experience with literally thousands of gangsters.

This first-hand experience in all phases of the illness is without warrant and highly treasured, in addition, recovery is of unparalleled, therapeutic value. We are here to share freely with any gangster who wants to live a crime free life. It is increasingly hard for ordinary citizens to grasp the complexities of issues related to a gangsters mentality. Sharing is one key to recovery. Any person currently involved in gang activities just cannot see it, but will. Those in need of healing will get it. Those in need of understanding will get it. This book is a standard reference guide for all serious about crime free living. Collaboration includes contribution by gangsters converted by a Higher Power, drug users healed by a Higher Power, productive citizens returned to society from prison by a Higher Power and the Higher Power in the heart of everyone inspired to contribute to these pages. Life recovered by a Higher Power. This G.A. Fellowship–approved effort is unlike any that came before it.

Who Is A Gangster?

Most of us do not have to think twice about this question. We know! Our whole way of life and thinking was the centered in a gangster's mentality in one form or another, banging, selling drugs, extorting money, robbery and murder and the list goes on. Street gang member or gangster means any person who actually and in fact belongs to a gang or criminal empire, whose goals is to extract finances through criminal means, and any person who knowingly acts in the capacity of an agent for or accessory to, or is legally accountable for, or voluntarily associates himself/herself with a course or pattern of gang related criminal activity, whether in preparatory, executor, or cover up phase of any activity, or who knowingly performs, aids, or abets any such activity. With the intent to provide the gang with any advantage in, or any control or dominance over any criminal market sector, including but not limited to, the manufacture, delivery, or sale of controlled substances or cannabis; arson or arson-for-hire, traffic in stolen property or stolen credit cards; traffic in prostitution, obscenity, or pornography; or that involves robbery, burglary, theft; or extortion professionally and sexually or having a common name or common identifying sign or symbol, and whose members individually or collectively engage in or have engaged in a pattern of criminal activity.

We loved to live "gangster." Very simply, a gangster is a man or woman whose life is ruled by criminal beliefs and actions. We are a people in the clutch of an on going and spreading mental illness whose end is always the same jails, institutions, and death. Those of us who have found the program of G.A. do not have to think twice about the question, "Who is a gangster?" We know! This is our experience. As gangsters, we are a people whose use of a criminal mentality in any form causes a problem in every area of our life. A gangster's mentality is an mental disorder which involves more than gang banging. It is caused by numerous reasons; for example, one may be exposure to an extreme traumatic occurrence. We in the fellowship of Gangsters Anonymous have all agreed that in most cases newcomers were involved in some form of actual or threatened death, serious injury or other threat to their life. Having discussed this with mental health professionals, most members do suffer from small to large forms of Post Traumatic Stress Disorder. Many believed as long as we were not gang banging, it was all right to live like gangsters. Some of us did not consider ourselves gangsters prior to coming to a G.A. meeting.

Female gangsters often live behind the iron curtain of their counterparts. They have hidden male gangsters from the law, and participated in every form of the gangster lifestyle. They suffer from the same mental attraction to this life as men but could not admit it to themselves. They may have the feeling that the embarrassment could be more than they could endure. Some may fear losing their children, jobs, or the respect of family and friends. In some cases, they shared their love for all things gangster with their children which led the child to prison, time and time again. They forced their friends and children to protect them from those they know they have harmed. By living life gangster the female gangster "unknown gangster" destroyed their kids chances at education, recreation and employment. Female gangsters live in homes under siege from themselves, their boyfriends and husbands. Our children were forced to live a life of horror and perversion at an early age. Until female gangsters found other women who had found a new way of life these "unknown gangsters" continued to feel hopeless and doomed to live the life of a gangster. The information available to us came from misinformed people.

As long as we could stop gang banging or thinking like gangsters "for a while", we thought we were all right .We looked at the "stopping" not the "thinking". As our gangster mentality progressed, we thought of stopping less and less. Only in desperation did we ask ourselves, "Could it be my thinking? In addition to having survived traumatic experiences, a gangster may exhibit symptoms of avoidance/numbing physiological arousal. The arousal symptoms may include insomnia, angry outbursts or irritability, and a general sense of jumpiness. Some did not choose to become gangsters and some did. We suffer from an illness that reveals itself in ways that make us social adversaries and that makes detection, prognosis and therapy difficult. Our illness isolated us from people except when we were drinking, smoking, hanging tough, selling drugs, selling sex and extortion or finding ways and means to make money illegally. Hostile, resentful, self-centered and self-seeking, we cut ourselves off from the outside world.

Anything not wholly well known became bizarre and dangerous to us. Our world shrank and isolation became our life. We used our gangster's mentality in order to survive. Some of us misused and abused people and still did not consider ourselves a gangster. Through all of this, we kept telling ourselves, "they are stupid and weak." Our misconceptions about the nature of a gangster included visions of violence, street crime, sexual and financial extortion, and jail. When our gangster mentality became a crime or moral deficiency, we became rebellious and fell deeper into isolation. Some of the highs felt great, but eventually the things we had to do to continue to "keep life gangster" mirrored desperation. We were caught in the embrace of our illness. We were forced to survive any way we could. We manipulated people and tried to control everything around us. We lied, stole, cheated, murdered, raped, and sold our selves.

Some female gangsters even used pregnancies to extort money knowing we had no intention of holding on to the relationship. We had to come up regardless of the cost. Failure and fear began to invade our life. One condition of our gangster mentality was our inability to deal with life on life's terms. We pit friends against friends, friends against family members, and family members against friends. We resented the obstacles society placed in our way. We lost the desire to run our own life. We gave our freedoms away at the drop of a hat. We used strong-arm tactics and combinations of assault and battery, intimidation, and finally, mayhem to cope with a seemingly hostile world. We dreamed of finding a magic formula that would solve our ultimate problem – ourselves. The fact is we could not be both honest and aggressive successfully.

A gangster's mentality ceased to make us feel good. At times, we were defensive about our gangster living and justified our right to gangbang or think like a gangster especially when we were unable to find employment. We were proud of the sometimes illegal and often bizarre behavior that typified our gangster's mentality. We only remembered the good times we had while living life gangster. At times, we sat alone and were consumed by fear and self-pity. We fell into a pattern of selective thinking. As original gangsters, some of us became larger than life. We owned the world (or so we thought). We justified and reasoned out the things we did to keep from living an impoverished life or to retaliate for unjustifiable homicides. We ignored the times when life seemed to be a nightmare. We avoided the reality of what a gangster represented. Higher mental and emotional functions such as conscience and the ability to love were sharply affected by our gangster mentality. Living skills were reduced to an animal level. Our spirit was broken. The capacity to feel human was lost.

This may seem extreme, but many of us have been in this state of mind. We were constantly searching for the answer that person, place, or thing that could make everything all right. We lacked the ability to cope with daily living. As we became more and more hard core, many of us found ourselves in and out of institutions. These experiences indicated that there was something wrong with our life. We began to notice the similarity between our gangsters mentality and anger. Many professionals have theorized that high levels of anger are related to a natural survival instinct. When initially confronted with extreme threat, anger is a normal response to terror, events that seem unfair, and feeling out of control or victimized. Many recovering gangsters experience these events still to this day. We wanted an easy way out. Some of us thought of suicide. Some of us became homicidal. We became a menace to our neighborhoods, communities and society, in general.

Our attempts at controlling were usually feeble and only helped to contribute to our feelings of worthlessness. We were trapped in the illusion of "what if?", and "if only" and "just one more time." When we searched or asked for help, we were only looking for the absence of pain. We had regained good reputations, we were newly released from prison, we displayed good behavior many times, only to lose it by applying a gangsters sense of reasoning an obstacle, to a normal life problem. Our record of accomplishment shows that it is impossible for us to "gangsterfie" life successfully. No matter how well we may appear to be in control, living a gangster's lifestyle always brings us to our knees. Like other fatal illnesses, a gangster's mentality can be cured. We agree that there is nothing shameful about being a gangster, provided we accept our predicament honestly and take positive action.

A better understanding was the idea that our prior mentality was abnormal and after our traumatic experience, our mentality led us to criminal behavior. We are willing to admit without reservation that we are vulnerable to this type of mentality. Common sense tells us that it would be insane to go back to the source of our vulnerability. Our experience indicates that medicine cannot cure our illness. Although physical and mental tolerance plays a role, the quality or level of our gangster mentality requires no extended period to trigger allergic reactions. Our direct response to this gangster mentality is what makes us gangster, not what we do once we begin, although the world suffers from our actions. Many of us did not think we had a problem with being a gangster or thinking like one, until we were shot, or a family member or friend was fatally wounded. It is common for trauma survivors to feel guilt, which can sometimes lead them to commit crimes that will likely result in their apprehension, punishment, serious injury, or death. Even when others told us we had a problem, we were convinced that we were right and the world was wrong. Some of us knew we were wrong but just did not have the desire to care.

We used this belief to justify our self-destructive behavior. We developed a point of view that enabled us to pursue our gangster mentality without concern for our own well-being or the well-being of others. We began to feel that our gangster's mentality was killing us long before we could ever admit it to anyone else. We noticed that if we tried to stop thinking like a gangster, we could not. We suspected that we had lost control over our thinking and had no power to remove those gangster thoughts from our minds. Certain things followed as we continued to think like a gangster. We became accustomed to a state of mind that is common to gangsters. We forgot what it was like before we began to think like gangsters. Some of us were taught this behavior while we were still in our pampers. If ever learned; we forgot about social graces. We acquired strange habits and mannerisms. If ever learned, we forgot how or refused to work. If ever learned, we forgot how or refused to play. If ever learned, we forgot how, refused to express ourselves, or were taught to express ourselves with sheer animal aggression. In addition, we showed no concern for others. We forgot how to feel.

While thinking like a gangster, we lived in another world. We experienced only periodic jolts of reality and self-awareness. It seemed that we were, at the very least, two people instead of one, Dr. Jekyll and Mr. Hyde. We ran around attempting to get our life together before making that next move. We have come to realize there are two moves possible. The right move or the smart move.

There are many men and women in prison after attempting to make the right moves in their lives. The most frequent move made in life is the right move. The right move isn't always the best move to make in life. We have found the smart move is much more difficult and much more rewarding. If the right thing to do is participate in an event, but the possibility of a crime occurring makes the right thing wrong. The smart move is to play the tape through to the end and decide to avoid the possibility of a crime occurring. Moral issues often cause many of our members to make the right choice rather than the smart choice. Sometimes we could do very well, but sometimes it was less important – and more impossible. In the end, Dr. Jekyll died and Mr. Hyde took over. Each of us has a few things that we never did. We cannot let these things become excuses to begin again. Some of us feel lonely because of differences between us and other members. This feeling makes it difficult to give up old connections and old habits. We all have different tolerances for pain. Some gangsters needed to go to greater extremes than others did. Some of us found we had enough when we realized that either most of our loved ones were dead or in jail and that, we were "gangstered out". This realization began to affect our daily life. At first, we were living a so-called "cool" gangster's life – a manner that seemed to be social or at least controllable.

We had little indication of the disaster that the future held for us. At some point, we became uncontrollable and anti-social. An emotional numbness came over us. The emotional numbness many gangsters experience can lead them to engage in sensation-seeking behavior in an attempt to experience some type of emotion. This began when things were going well, and we were in situations that allowed us frequent gangster thoughts and responses. This is usually the end of the good times. We may have tried to moderate, substitute or even control our gangster's mentality but we went from a state of straight success and well-being to complete spiritual, mental and emotional bankruptcy. This rate of decline varies from gangster to gangster. Whether it occurs in years or days, it is downhill.

Those of us who do not die from the ill thinking will go on to prison, mental institutions, or complete demoralization as the ill thinking progresses. Gangster life had given us the feeling that we could handle whatever situation might develop. We became aware, however, that a gangster's mentality was largely responsible for some of our worst predicaments. Some of us may spend the rest of our life in jail for a crime induced by a gangster thought. We had to reach our bottom before we were willing to stop. We were finally motivated to seek help in the latter stage of our living with a gangster's reality. Then it was easier for us to see the destruction, disaster, and delusion of a gangster and the thoughts that follow. It was harder to deny our lifestyle when problems were staring us in the face. Some of us first saw the effects of our lifestyle on the people closest to us. Our little brothers and sisters began to mimic our dangerous behavior in some cases, our children. We were very dependent on our family or on our gangster friends to carry us through life. We felt angry, disappointed and hurt when they found other interests, friends, and loved ones. Our lifestyles enslaved us. We were prisoners of our own mind, and were condemned by our own guilt.

We gave up the hope that we would ever stop committing crimes or thinking like a gangster. Our attempts to stay straight always failed, causing us pain and misery. As gangsters, we have an incurable illness centered in our thinking. The illness is chronic, progressive and most often fatal. However, it is a treatable illness. We begin to treat our thinking by not using a gangster solution to an everyday life problem. Many of us sought answers but failed to find any workable solution until we found each other. Once we identified ourselves as gangsters, help became possible. We can see a little of ourselves in every gangster and see a little of them in us. This insight lets us help one another. Our future seemed hopeless until we found crime free men and women. The people in the G.A. meeting told us that they were recovering gangsters who had learned to live without committing crimes and gangster solutions. If they could do it, so could we.

The only alternatives to recovery are jails, institutions, dereliction, or death. Unfortunately, our lifestyle makes us deny our thinking. If you are a gangster, you can find a new way of life through the G.A. meeting. We have become very grateful in the course of our recovery. Through abstinence and working through this process, our life have, for certain, become useful. We realize that we are never cured and that we carry this thinking within us for the rest of our life. We have an illness but we can and do recover. We regret the past, dreaded the future, and we were not too thrilled about the present. After years of searching, we were unhappy and less satisfied than when it all began. Our future seemed hopeless until we found recovering gangsters who live crime free and who were willing to share with us. Denial of our gangster lifestyle kept us sick but our honest admission of a gangster life enabled us to stop living life as a gangster.

What Is The Gangsters Anonymous Program?

G.A. is a non-profit fellowship or society of men and women for whom a gangster's mentality had become a major problem. We are recovering gangsters who meet regularly to help each other stay "Crime free". This is a meeting of complete abstinence from all things gangster. There is only one requirement for membership, the desire to arrest our gangster mentality. We suggest that you keep an open mind and give yourself a break. Our program is a set of principles written so simply that they can be followed in our daily life. The most important thing about them is that they work.

There are no strings attached to G.A. We are not

affiliated with any other organizations. We have no initiation fees or dues, no pledges to sign, no promises to make to anyone. We are not connected with any political, religious, or law enforcement groups, and are under no surveillance at any time. Anyone may join us, regardless of age, race, sexual identity, creed, religion, or lack of religion. We are not interested in what or how big you became or what set you were from, what you have done in the past, how much or how little you have, but only in what you want to do about your problem and how we can help. The Newcomer is the most important person at any meeting, because we can only keep what we have by giving it away.

G.A. is a fellowship of men and women who are learning to live without gang life or a gangster's mentality which normally results in criminal behavior. We are a non-profit society and have no dues or fees of any kind. Each of us has paid the price of membership. We have paid the right to recover with our pain. Surviving against all odds, we are gangsters who meet regularly. We respond to honest sharing and listen to the stories of our members for the message of recovery. We realize that there is hope for us at last. We make use of the tools that have worked for other recovering gangsters who have learned in G.A. to live without gang life or a gangster's mentality or criminal behavior. The Twelve Steps are positive tools that make our recovery possible. Our primary purpose is to stay "Crime Free" and in some cases, "Gangster Free", and to carry the message to the gangster who stills suffers. We are united by our common problem of gang life and a gangster's mentality. By meeting, talking, and helping other gangsters, we are able to stay "Crime free". We have learned from our experiences that those who keep coming to our meetings regularly stay "Crime-Free".

G.A. has many years of experience with literally hundreds of thousands of gangsters. This first-hand experience in all phases of illness and recovery is of unparalleled, therapeutic value. We are here to share freely with any gangster who wants to recover. Our message of recovery is based on our experience. Before coming to the Fellowship, we exhausted ourselves by trying to change our lifestyles and wondering what was wrong with us. After coming to G.A., we found ourselves among a very special group of people who have suffered like us and found recovery. In their experiences, freely shared, we found hope for ourselves. If the meeting worked for them, it would work for us. The only requirement for membership is a desire to stop thinking like a gangster. We have seen the program work for any gangster who honestly and sincerely wants to stop. We do not have to be "crime-free" when we first come to a meeting, but after the first meeting, we suggest that members keep coming back and come back crime-free. We don't have to wait for a brush with death or a jail sentence to get help from G.A. A criminal lifestyle is not a hopeless condition from which there is no recovery. We meet gangsters like ourselves who are crime free. We watch, listen and realize they have found a way to live and enjoy life without gang life or a gangster's mentality. We do not have to settle for limitations of the past.

We can examine and re-examine our old ideas. We can constantly improve our old ideas or replace them with new ones. We are men and women who have discovered and admitted that we are powerless over gang life and the gangster's mentality, which grows from it. When we gangbang or think like a gangster, we lose. When we discovered that we could not live with or without gang life or the thinking associated, we sought help through G.A. rather than prolong our suffering. The program works a miracle in our life. We become different people. Working the steps and maintaining abstinence gives us a daily reprieve from our self-imposed life sentences.

We become free to live. We want our place of recovery to be a safe place free from outside influences. For the protection of the Fellowship, we insist that no "Rags", flyers, pamphlets or guns be brought to any meeting. We feel very free to express ourselves within the Fellowship because law enforcement agencies are not involved. Our meetings have an atmosphere of empathy. In accordance with the principles of recovery, we try not to judge, stereotype, or moralize with each other. We are not recruited and membership does not cost anything. G.A. does not provide counseling or social services. Our meetings are a process of identification, hope, and sharing. The heart of G.A. beats when two gangsters share their recovery. What we do becomes real for us when we share it. This happens on a larger scale in our regular meetings. A meeting happens when two or more gangsters gather to help each other stay crime free. At the beginning of the meeting, we read the G.A. literature that is available to anyone. Some meetings have speakers, topic discussions or both. Closed meetings are for gangsters or those who think they might suffer from a gangster's mentality. Open meetings welcome anyone wishing to experience our fellowship.

The atmosphere of recovery is protected by our Twelve Traditions. We are fully self-supporting through voluntary contributions from our members. Regardless of where the meeting takes place, we remain unaffiliated. Meetings provide a place to be with fellow gangsters. All we need are two gangsters, caring and sharing, to make a meeting. We let new ideas flow into us. We ask questions. We share what we have learned about living without gang life and the associated thinking. However, the principles of the Twelve Steps may seem strange to us at first. The most important thing about them is they work. Our meeting is a way of life.

We learn the value of spiritual principles such as surrender, humility and service from reading the G.A. literature going to meetings and working the Steps. We find that our life steadily improve if we maintain abstinence from crime and a gangsters mentality and work the Twelve Steps to sustain our recovery. Living this program gives us a relationship with a Power greater than ourselves, corrects defects and leads us to help others. Where there has been wrong, the program teaches us the spirit of forgiveness.

Many books have been written about the life of a gangster. This book concerns itself with the nature of recovery. If you are a gangster and have found this book, please, give yourself a break and read it.

The Twelve Traditions of G.A.

We keep what we have only with dedication, and just as freedom for the individual come from the Twelve Steps, so freedom for the group springs from our traditions. As long as the ties that bind us together are stronger than those that would tear us apart, all will be well.

1.   Our common welfare should come first; personal recovery depends on G.A. unity.

2.   For our group purpose there is but one ultimate authority – a loving Higher Power as He may express   Himself in our group conscience. Our leaders are but trusted servants, they do not govern.

3.   The only requirement for membership is a desire to stop committing crimes.

4.   Each group should be autonomous except in

matters affecting other groups or G.A. as a whole.

5.	Each group has but one primary purpose–to carry the message to the gangster who still suffers.

6.	A G.A. group ought never endorse, finance, or lend the G.A. name to any related facility or outside enterprise, lest problems of money, property, or prestige divert us from our primary purpose.

7.	Every G.A. group ought to be fully self-supporting, declining outside contributions.

8.	G.A. should remain forever nonprofessional, but our service centers may employ special workers.

9.	G.A., as such, ought never to be organized, but we may create service boards or committees directly responsible to those they serve.

10.	G.A. has no opinion on outside issues; hence, the G.A. name ought never to be drawn into public controversy.

11.	Our public relations policy is based on attraction rather than promotion; we need always maintain personal anonymity at the level of press, radio, and films.

12.	Anonymity is the spiritual foundation of all our traditions, ever reminding us to place principles before personalities.

Keep Coming Back

Before coming to the Fellowship of G.A., we could

not manage our own life. We could not live and enjoy life as other people do. We had to have something different and we thought we had found it in gang life. We placed our gangster life and a gangster's mentality ahead of the welfare of our families, our wives, husbands, and our children. We taught our children suicidal ways of walk, talk, and how to react like gangsters. In some cases, we even dressed them this way. We had to be surrounded by gangsters at all costs. We did many people great harm but most of all, we harmed ourselves.

Through our inability to accept personal responsibilities, we were actually creating our own problems. We seemed incapable of facing life on its own terms. Most of us realized that representing a gang could get us killed. We were slowly committing suicide, but a gangster's mentality is such a cunning enemy of life that we had lost the power to do anything about it. Many of us ended up in jail, or sought help through medicine, religion, and psychiatry. None of these methods were sufficient for us. Our love to keep it gangster resurfaced or continued to progress until, in desperation, we sought help from each other in G.A.

After coming to G.A., we realized we were sick people. We suffered from an illness from which there is no known cure. It can, however, be arrested at some point, and recovery is then possible. We are gangsters seeking recovery. We used a gangster's mentality to cover our feelings and did whatever was necessary to keep the rituals of the criminal atmosphere.

Many of us were stabbed or shot, unable to make it to work, or went to work ready to stab or shoot someone. Many of us stole whatever we could to provide our worthiness. We hurt the ones we love. We did all these things and told ourselves, "I can handle it". We were looking for a way out. We could not face life on life's terms. In the beginning, being with a gang was fun. For us a gangster's mentality became a habit and finally was necessary for survival. The progression of the illness was not apparent to us. We continued on the part of destruction, unaware of where it was leading us. We were gangsters for life and did not know it.

Through gang life, we tried to avoid reality, pain and misery. When our friends would die or be imprisoned, we realized we had those same problems, and they were becoming worse. We sought relief through retaliation, extortion, and robbery more and more often. We sought help and found none. Often parole agents could not understand our dilemma. They tried to help by giving us programs, which only fueled our insanity. We began to abscond. Our whereabouts became unknown. Our wives, husbands and loved ones gave us what they had and drained themselves in the hope that we would stop living the life of a gangster and get better. We tried substituting our criminal lifestyle with drugs, women, and men this only prolonged our pain. We tried limiting our involvement to social outings such as house parties and barbecues without success. There is no such thing as a social gangster. Some of us sought an answer through churches, religions or cults.

Some sought a cure by geographical change. We blamed our surroundings and living situations for our problems. This attempt to cure our problems by moving gave us a chance to take advantage of new people. Some of us sought approval through sex or change of friends. This approval-seeking behavior carried us further into our gangster's mentality. Some of us tried marriage, divorce, or desertion. Regardless of what we tried, we could not escape from our gangster mentality and ways.

We reached a point in our life where we felt like a lost cause. We had little worth to family, friends, or on the job. Many of us were unemployed and unemployable. Any form of success was frightening and unfamiliar. We did not know what to do. As the feeling of self-loathing grew, we needed to be hardcore to mask our feelings.

We were sick and tired of pain and trouble; we were frightened and hid our fear. No matter to what limit we would hide our fear, we always carried fear with us. We were hopeless, useless, and lost. Failure had become our way of life and self-esteem was non existent. Perhaps the most painful feeling of all was the desperation. Isolation and denial of our lifestyle kept us moving this downhill path. Any hope of getting better disappeared. Helplessness emptiness and fear became our way of life. We were complete failures. Personality change was what we really needed. Change from self-destructive patterns of life became necessary. When we lied, cheated or stole, we degraded ourselves in our own eyes. We had enough of self-destruction. We experienced our powerlessness.

When nothing relieved our paranoia and fear, we hit bottom and became ready to ask for help. We were searching for an answer when we reached out and found G.A. We came to our first G.A. meeting in defeat and did not know what to expect. After sitting in a meeting, we began to feel that people cared and were willing to help. Although our minds told us that we would never make it, the people in the Fellowship gave us hope by insisting that we could recover. We found that no matter what our past thought or actions were, others had felt and done the same. Surrounded by fellow gangsters, we realized that we were not alone anymore. Recovery is what happens in our meetings. Our life is at stake. We found that by putting recovery first, the G.A. meeting works. We faced three disturbing realizations: One-we were powerless over this gangster's mentality and two our life had become unmanageable and three although we were not responsible for our illness, we are responsible for our recovery. We can no longer blame people, places, and things for our gangster ways. We must face our problems and our feelings. The ultimate weapon for recovery is the recovering gangster. We concentrate on recovery and feelings – not what we have done in the past.

Old friends, places, and ideas are often a threat to our recovery. We need to change our playmates, playgrounds and playthings. When we realize that we are not able to manage without a gangster twist, some of us immediately begin to experience depression, anxiety, hostility, and resentment. Petty frustrations, minor setbacks and loneliness often make us feel that we are not getting any better. We find that we suffer from an illness, not a moral dilemma. We were critically ill, not hopelessly bad. Our illness can only be arrested through abstinence.

Today, we experience a full range of feelings. Before coming into the Fellowship, we felt either elated or depressed. Our negative sense of self has been replaced by a positive concern for others. Answers are provided, and problems are solved. It is a great gift to feel human again. What a change from the way we used to be! We know the G.A. Meeting works. The meeting convinced us that we needed to change ourselves, instead of trying to change the people and situations around us. We discovered new opportunities. We found a sense of self-worth. We learned self-respect. This is a meeting for learning. By working the Steps, we come to accept God's Will. Acceptance leads to recovery. We lose our fear of the unknown. We are set free.

This Is How We Do It

How we got into this lifestyle and way of thinking is of no immediate importance to us. We are concerned with recovery. If you want what we have to offer, and are willing to make the effort to get it, then you are ready to take certain steps. These are the principles that made our recovery possible:

1.   We admitted that we were powerless over our gangster mentality and that our life had become unmanageable.

2.   We came to believe that a Power greater than ourselves could restore us to sanity.

3.   We made a decision to turn our will and our life over to the care of God, as we understood Him.

4.   We made a searching and fearless moral inventory of ourselves.

5.   We admitted to God, to ourselves, and to another human being the exact nature of our wrongs.

6.   We were entirely ready to have God remove all

these defects of character.

7.   We humbly asked Him to remove all these defects of character.

8.   We made a list of all persons we had harmed, and became willing to make amends to them all.

9.   We made direct amends to such people wherever possible, except when to do so would injure them or others.

10.   We continued to take personal inventory and when we were wrong promptly admitted it.

11.   We sought through prayer and meditation to improve our conscious contact with God, as we understood Him, praying only for knowledge of His Will for us and the Power to carry that out.

12.   Having had a spiritual awakening as a result of these steps, we carried this message to the still suffering gangsters, and practiced these principles in all our affairs.

This may sound impossible, and there is no way we can do it all at once. We did not become gangsters in one day, so remember-easy does it? There is one thing more than anything else that will defeat us in our recovery; this is an attitude of indifference or intolerance toward spiritual principles. Three of these that are indispensable are honesty, open-mindedness, and willingness. We know that this is a new means of reaching this gangster mentality and viewing it in a real way. One gangster helping another gangster see the reality of what, where, and how this thinking can harm us in so many ways.

We know how difficult this will be. We feel one gangster can best describe to another what it takes to get up to and through and then finally past our thinking; and become what we would like to become that is productive members of our families, friends and community in general. We know if we stand face to face with our thinking without fear we can quickly reach the goal of becoming respected, responsible, and appreciated men and women in our society. The way to stay away from all things gangster is to eliminate these things as quickly as possible, but first you must identify them in your own terms, through what and how you created them. Each one of us has our own manifestation of the things we know to be gangster. So we know just for today we cannot mentally go there.

If you are like many of us, you know that once it is on... it is on! We have to say this because we know once that thought pops in our heads we release our obsession for all things gangster. Once this happens we lose our will to care. Something we cannot afford to participate in is an unfeeling and uncaring state, a zombie like condition. Thinking of players, pimps, and hustlers as well as call girls, prostitutes and hoes as anything other than gangster has confused many of us and caused much harm in our life. We cannot ignore the fact that these subtitles are all gangsterfied. It takes true a true understanding and an honest self-evaluation to admit this and move on. We are a people with the need to gangsterfy life. We must abstain from all things criminal in order to recover.

These are some of the questions we asked ourselves: Are we sure we want to stop living life gangster? Do we understand that we have no real control over our gangsters mentality? Do we recognize that in the end, we did not use gangsters–they used us? Did jail and institutions take over the management of our life at different times? Do we fully accept the fact that our every attempt to stop thinking likes gangsters or to control our criminal thoughts failed? Do we know that our involvement in the mentality changed us into someone we did not want to be, dishonest, self–willed, and deceitful, people at odds with our fellow man and ourselves? Do we really believe that we have failed as gangsters? When we were living with a gangster's mentality, reality became so painful that oblivion was preferable. We tried to keep other people from knowing our pain. We were afraid to let anyone know we had this deep secret. We isolated ourselves, and lived in prisons that we built with loneliness. Through this desperation, we sought help in Gangsters Anonymous. When we come to G.A., we are physically, mentally, and spiritually bankrupt. Probation and parole seemed unending. We have lost very dear loved ones. We have hurt so long that we are willing to go to any length to stay crime free. Our only hope is to live by the example of those who have faced our dilemma and have found a way out. Regardless of who we are and where we came.

We have found we had no choice except in completely changing our old ways of thinking or go back to gangster life. When we give our best, it works for us as it has worked for others. When we could no longer stand our old ways, we began to change. From that point forward, we began to see that every crime free day is a successful day, no matter what happens. Surrender means not having to fight anymore. We accept our gangster mentality and life the way it is. We become willing to do whatever is necessary to stay crime free, even the things we do not like doing. Until we took Step 1, we were full of fear and doubt. At this point, many of us felt lost and confused. We felt different. Upon working this step, we affirmed our surrender to the principles of G.A. Only after surrender are we able to overcome the alienation of this gangster's mentality. Help for the gangster begins only when we are able to admit complete defeat. This can be frightening. Step One means that we do not have to live like a gangster, and this is a great freedom. It took a while for some of us to realize that our life had become unmanageable. For others, the unmanageability of their life was the only thing crystal clear. We knew in our hearts that a gangster's mentality had the power to change us into someone we did not want to be.

Being crime-free and working this step, we grow helpful. However, none of the steps works by magic. We do not just say the words of this step; we learn to live them. We see for ourselves that the meeting has something to offer us. We have found hope. We can learn to function in the world in which we live. We can find meaning and purpose in life from insanity, depravity and death. When we admit our powerlessness and inability to manage our own life, we open the door for a Power greater than us to help us. It is not where we were that counts, but where we are going.

STEP ONE:

"We admitted we were powerless over our gangster mentality and our life had become unmanageable".

Many of us tried to stop thinking like gangsters on sheer willpower. This action was a temporary solution. We saw that willpower alone would not work for any length of time. We tried countless other remedies – psychiatrists, hospitals, recovery houses, lovers, new towns, new jobs. Everything we tried, failed. We began to see that we had rationalized the most outrageous sort of nonsense to justify the mess that we made of our life with our gangster mentality.

As a direct result of our choices, conditions, and the choices of our guardians we unfortunately have found ourselves in an atmosphere plagued with a criminal disease. Unlike many in the same environment we unfortunately contracted the disease in a major way. As we displayed its symptoms, we began to find ourselves wrongfully charged, in and out of jail. There are those whose disease never developed aggressively. They are the fortunate ones. The Code is a symptom of this incredibly contagious criminal mentality. Its signs are known to bring pain and in some cases death. Our members have studied this symptom heavily and have come to find the only cure is avoidance. Our solution is very simple but difficult for most. Our experiences suggest we remove ourselves mentally from the code. We learn to cut the apron strings we have with others actively participating in this disease. Visiting the contagious area periodically can cause serious negative results. Curiosity of what goes on while we are away can be suicidal. Our awareness of the code is our defense against its wrath. When it appears we remove ourselves from its area. Our cure comes with time and a reputation of avoidance. As long as we stay crime free and keep our distance from those committing crimes, our chances of becoming a victim of it diminishes. We are street poisoned individuals searching for the antidote and a crime free life.

Until we remove our resentments, no matter what they are, the foundation of our recovery is in danger. Resentments rob us of the benefits this meeting has to offer. In ridding ourselves of all resentments, we surrender. Then, and only then, can we be helped to recover from the illness of this gangster mentality. Now, the question is: "If we are powerless, how can Gangsters Anonymous help?" We begin by asking for help. The foundation of our program is the admission that we, of ourselves, do not have power to control this gangster mentality. When we can accept this fact, we have completed the first part of Step One.

We then begin to practice spiritual principles. Honesty being the first spiritual principle. When we step into the rooms we feel out of place. We feel we are selling our cliques or way of life out. However, if we were to search deeper within we would see the positive representation of our past experiences in what we are doing with our lives today. We must learn to be ok with a simple life in the beginning of our recovery. We will get stares and negative vibes from our friends. They love you and miss the man or girl they remember. Who will they brag about knowing. We reciprocate the love and continue on our journey. Hoping one day we will save them a seat at the table of growth and spiritual awareness. Once again we begin our First Step, we should begin to ask ourselves a few basic questions. Can I learn how not to walk talk fight rob and love this way of life? Am I willing to stop living life criminally? Am I willing to do whatever it takes to recover from this destructive way of live. When the choice appears, G.A. or our old way we begin to see the appeal. Letting go of our reservation is most important, especially the ones that rob us of our ability to surrender to our new way of life. The sooner we identify our reservations, the sooner we can we can begin the process of elimination. Reservations can be anything...a belief that we don't really have a problem. Placing conditions on our crime removing ideas. Staying crime free only while we have a job or someone is giving us a place to stay. By working the steps we learn to carry our thug free life as strong as we carried our active gangster life. Another reservation would be continuing to hang with the people still associated with criminal behavior. It doesn't always have to be a past associate. There will be new choices and faces that appear cool and good but we must use our acquired street sense to recognize poisonous people and their strategies. Another reservation is working only certain steps. Saying to ourselves, " I'll work Step 3 but I won't work Step 4. Finding ways to overcome our reservations will become easier when we look to other recovering gangsters for help.

A second admission must be made before our foundation is complete. If we stop here, we will know only half the truth. We are great ones for manipulating the truth. We say on one hand, "Yes, I am powerless over my gangster mentality;" and on the other hand, "When I get my life together, I can handle a gangster mentality." Such thoughts and actions led us to believe that a gangster mentality is an asset. It never occurred to us to ask, "If we can't control our gangster mentality, how can we control our life?" We felt miserable without the gangster life, and our life had become unmanageable.

Unemployment, dereliction and destructiveness are easily seen as characteristics of an unmanageable life. Our families are generally disappointed, baffled and confused by our gangster living and often desert or disown us. Becoming employed, socially acceptable and reunited with our families does not make our life manageable. Social acceptability does not equal recovery. We have found we had no choice except completely change our old ways of thinking or go back to gangster life. When we give our best, it works for us as it has worked for others. When we could no longer stand our old ways, we began to change. From that point forward, we began to see that every crime free day is a successful day, no matter what happens.

Surrender means not having to fight anymore. We accept our gangster mentality and life the way it is. We become willing to do whatever is necessary to stay crime free, even the things we don't like doing. Until we took Step One, we were full of fear and doubt. At this point, many of us felt lost and confused. We felt different. Upon working this step, we affirmed our surrender to the principles of G.A. Only after surrender are we able to overcome the alienation of this gangsters' mentality. Help for the gangster begins only when we are able to admit complete defeat. This can be frightening, but it is the foundation on which we built our life.

Step One means that we do not have to live like a gangster, and this is a great freedom. It took a while for some of us to realize that our life had become unmanageable. For others, the unmanageability of their life was the only thing clear. We knew in our hearts that a gangsters' mentality had the power to change us into someone we didn't want to be. Being crime free and working this step, we are released from our chains. However, none of the steps work by magic. We do not just say the words of this step; we learn to live them. We see for ourselves that the meeting has something to offer us.

We have found hope. We can learn to function in the world in which we live. We can find meaning and purpose in life and be rescued from insanity, depravity and death. When we admit our powerlessness and inability to manage our own life, we open the door for a Power greater than ourselves to help us. It is not where we were that counts, but where we are going.

Everyone hates to admit when the jig is up. Most people of course in the beginning fight this reality. Every natural instinct cries out against the idea of personal powerlessness. It is truly awful to admit that, fully gangstered out, we have warped our minds into such an obsession to commit crimes that only an act of divine intervention can remove it from us.

No other kind of bankruptcy is like this one. Someone has unleashed an unsettling piece of information which now shows how crime becomes the greedy creditor, bleeds us of all self sufficiency and all will to resist its demands. Psychologists have a term for this, Post Traumatic Stress Syndrome. They have come to a realization that most criminals have lived through some type of traumatic experience. This experience was the catalyst to their contraction of a mental disorder simply known as a criminal mentality. Once this stark fact is understood, our bankruptcy of having human concerns will be no more.

After entering recovery we begin to take a different opinion of this embarrassing mental disorder. We become convinced that only through waving the white flag are we able to take our first steps toward freedom and justice and the cure. Our admissions of personal powerlessness finally turn out to be firm bricks upon which happy and purposeful life may be built.

We know that little good can come to any gangster who joins G.A. unless he has first accepted his devastating weakness and all its consequences. Until he so humbles himself, his crime free life, if any, will be insecure. Of real happiness he will find none at all. Proved beyond doubt by immense experience, this is one of the facts of being a recovering gangster. The principle that we shall find no enduring strength until we first admit complete defeat, the main tap root from which our whole Society has sprung and flowered.

When first challenged to admit defeat, most of us revolted. We approached recovery expecting to be taught self confidence. Then we had been told that so far as a gangsters' mentality is concerned, self confidence was no good whatsoever; in fact, it was a total liability. Our sponsors declared that we were the victims of a mental obsession so subtly powerful that no amount of human willpower could break it. There was, they said, no such thing as the personal conquest of this compulsion by the unaided will. Relentlessly deepening our dilemma, our sponsors pointed out our increasing sensitivity to crime, an allergy, they called it. We quite often break out in handcuffs and prison bars. The tyrant gangsters' mentality wielded a double edged sword over us: first we were struck by an insane urge that condemned us to go on committing crimes, and then by an allergy of the mind that insured we would ultimately destroy ourselves in the process. Few indeed were those who, so assailed, had ever won in single handed combat. It was a statistical fact that gangsters almost never recovered on their own resources. And this had been true, apparently, ever since man had first begun committing crimes.

In Gangsters Anonymous' pioneering time, none but the most desperate cases could swallow and digest this unacceptable truth. Even these "last gaspers" often had difficulty in realizing how hopeless they actually were. But a few did, and when they laid hold of recovering principles with all the fervor with which the drowning seize life preservers, they almost invariably got well. That is why the first edition of the book "Gangsters Anonymous," being published while our membership is small, deals with low bottom cases only. Many less desperate gangsters tried recovery, but did not succeed because they could not make the admission of hopelessness.

It is a tremendous satisfaction to record that in the following years this changed. Many recovering gangsters who still had their health, their families, their jobs, and even two cars in the garage, began to recognize their gangster mentality. As this trend grew, they were joined by young people who were scarcely more than potential gangsters. They were spared that last ten or fifteen years of literal hell the rest of us had gone through. Since Step One requires an admission that our life have become unmanageable, how could people such as these take this Step? It was obviously necessary to raise the bottom the rest of us had hit to the point where it would hit them. By going back in our own criminal histories, we could show that years before we realized it we were out of control, that our criminal behavior even then was no mere habit, that it was indeed the beginning of a fatal progression. To the doubters we could say, "Perhaps you're not a gangster/criminal after all. Why don't you try some more controlled crime, bearing in mind meanwhile what we have told you about a gangster mentality?" This attitude brought immediate and practical results. **It was then discovered that when one gangster plants in the mind of another the true nature of his malady, that person could never be the same again.** Following every spree, he would say to himself, "Maybe those recovering gangster's were right. . . ." After a few such experiences, often years before the onset of extreme difficulties, he would return to us convinced. He had hit bottom as truly as any of us. Scarface himself had become our best advocate.

Why all this insistence that every recovering gangster must hit bottom first? The answer is that few people will sincerely try to practice the G.A. program unless they have hit bottom. For practicing members of the fellowship the remaining eleven steps means the adoption of attitudes and actions that almost no gangster who is still committing crimes can dream of having. Who wishes to be rigorously honest and tolerant? Who wants to confess his faults to another and make restitution for harm done? Who cares anything about a Higher Power, let alone meditation and prayer? Who wants to sacrifice time and energy in trying to carry G.A's message to the next gangster? No, the average gangster, self centered in the extreme, doesn't care for this prospect unless he has to do these things in order to stay alive himself. Under the lash of a gangster mentality, we are driven to recovery, and there we discover the fatal nature of our situation. Then, and only then, do we become as open minded to conviction and as willing to listen as the dying can be. We stand ready to do anything which will lift the merciless obsession from us.

STEP TWO

"We came to believe that a Power greater than ourselves could restore us to sanity."

The Second Step is necessary if we expect to achieve ongoing recovery. The First Step leaves us with a need to believe in something that can help us with our powerlessness, uselessness, and helplessness. The First Step has left a vacuum in our life. We need to find something to fill that void. This is the purpose of the Second Step. Some of us didn't take this step seriously at first; we passed over it with a minimum of concern, only to find the next steps would not work until we worked Step Two. Even when we admitted that, we needed help with our gangster problem, many of us would not admit to the need for faith and sanity.

We have an illness: progressive, incurable and fatal. One way or another we went out and bought our destruction on the time payment plan! The most obvious insanity of the illness of gangster living is the obsession to hurt ourselves and/or others. Ask yourself this question, Do I believe it would be insane to walk up to someone and say, "I am a real gangster ...shoot me." If you can agree that this would be an insane thing, you should have no problem with the Second Step. In this meeting, the first thing we do is stop committing crimes. At this point, we begin to feel the pain of living without gangster life or anything to replace it. The pain forces us to seek a Power greater than ourselves that can relieve our obsession to think like a gangster. The process of coming to believe is similar for most gangsters.

Most of us lacked a working relationship with a Higher Power. We begin to develop this relationship by simply admitting to the possibility of a Power greater than us. Most of us have no trouble admitting that gangster living had become a destructive force in our life. Our best efforts resulted in even greater destruction and despair. At some point, we realized that we needed the help of some Power greater than our gangster living did. Our understanding of a Higher Power is up to us. No one is going to decide for us. We can call it the group, the program, or we can call it God. The only suggested guidelines are that this Power be loving, caring and greater than we are. We do not have to be religious to accept this idea. The point is that we open our minds to believe. We may have difficulty with this, but by keeping an open mind, eventually, we find the help we need. We talked and listened to others.

As we see coincidences and miracles happening in our life, acceptance becomes trust. We grow to feel comfortable with our Higher Power as a source of strength. As we learn to trust this Power, we begin to overcome our fear of life. The process of coming to believe restores us to sanity. The strength to move into action comes from this belief. We need to accept this step to start on the road to recovery. When our belief has grown, we are ready for Step 3. The moment they read Step Two, most recovering gangster newcomers are confronted with a dilemma, sometimes a serious one. How often have we heard them cry out, "Look what you people have done to us! You have convinced us that we are gangsters and that our life are unmanageable. Having reduced us to a state of absolute helplessness, you now declare that none but a Higher Power can remove our obsession. Some of us *won't* believe in God, others can't, and still others who do believe that

God exists have no faith whatsoever He will perform this miracle. Yes, you've got us over the barrel all right, but where do we go from here?"

Let's look first at the case of the one who says he won't believe the square one. He is in a state of mind which can be described only as savage. His whole philosophy of life, in which he so glorified, is threatened. It's bad enough, he thinks, to admit a gangsters mentality has him down for keeps. But now, still smarting from that admission, he is faced with something really impossible. How he does cherish the thought the gangster, risen so majestically from a single cell in the developed ooze, is the spearhead of evolution and therefore the only god that his universe knows! Must he renounce all this to save himself? At this juncture, the recovering gangster's sponsor usually laughs. This, the Newcomer thinks, is just about the last straw. This is the beginning of the end. And so it is: the beginning of the end of his old life, and the beginning of his emergence into a new one. His sponsor probably says, "Take it easy. The hoop you have to jump through is a lot wider than you think. At least I've found it so. So did a friend of mine who was a one time vice president of the American Atheist Society, but he got through with room to spare." "Well," says the newcomer, "I know you're telling me the truth. It's no doubt a fact that G. A. is full of people who once believed as I do. But just how, in these circumstances, does a fellow 'take it easy'? That's what I want to know." "That," agrees the sponsor, "is a very good question indeed. I think I can tell you exactly how to relax.

You won't have to work at it very hard, either.

We believed if we found a "legal hustle" or stopped hanging with our crime partners, or changed our living arrangements or found a job our lives would improve. These ideas consistently failed us, but we continued to hold on to them. We managed to elude our family and friends with the idea that we were not involved in the gangster thing. Although all evidence showed we were in with both feet. We often lied to ourselves by saying we were only trying to pay our mothers bills. We were involved because we were being picked. We had every excuse in the book. The simple reason we were involved was fear. Fear being alone. Fear of letting our family down. Fears that could easily be eliminated with support square friends and family. We were afraid to ask and in most cases when we did ask the response was nill. Until we found other men and women who feared what we feared but found constructive legal and honest solutions. Let's remember.. whatever problem arises in life there is a simple honest solution. It may be hard to reach but what riches are there that is easy to achieve legally. None. Sweat and tears are the exercise of the day. We denied we had a problem with this gangster mentality. We justified our actions, despite the wreckage around us. The Spiritual side of our illness, the side we often identify is the loneliness and that internal emptiness. This is reasonably the most troubling side of this gangster mind set because of its deep effect on most of us , we sometimes find it difficult to apply a program of recovery to it. We must remember No One changes overnight.

SEEK THE NEED FOR CHANGE, BUT NEVER REFORM TOO MUCH AT ONCE

Everyone understands the need for change in the abstract, but on the day-to-day level people are creatures of habit. Too much innovation is traumatic, and will lead to revolt. If you are new to a position of change, or an outsider trying to build a new reality, make a show of respecting the squares way of doing things. If change is necessary make it feel like a gentle improvement on the past.

Looking back at the problems created by our I'll thinking one thing proven beyond a reasonable doubt, was the fact that our life unsafe and lacked societies acceptance. We lived below the surface of mankind. We wanted desperately to be of this earth and recognized as one if it's loving earthly caring beings. By seeing all the things out of place with our *life* this becomes a true reality. Although, we manifest our gangsters mentality in our own destructive ways, many recovering gangsters tell about the signs they began to see before coming to G.A. Signs of guilt and uncontrolled emotions. Some of us are orphans raised by the system. Some are new to America and struggling to feed ourselves and family. Many of us are addicted to legal and illegal drugs. We are the offspring of career criminals. This mental disorder attracts even the affluent. We are often the only individuals never taught to function in the natural order of things. We in some cases, have spent many years in prisons and drug rehabilitation programs. We were often able to achieve sobriety yet never able to walk in the form of a Non gangster. We have lived through death defying experiences. Whatever our one on one experience, we were driven by selfishness, uncontrolled neediness and obsession. It was all grouped together sending us into destructive and often violent activities.

Maybe we were uncertain about the role our mentality played in our life before coming to Gangsters Anonymous meetings. Our self centeredness clouded our view of who we were. It wasn't until we arrived into the rooms of G. A. ; we realized how bad our lives were. Although some experienced enormous success criminally we our gangsters mentality destroyed all that it created. We can't fool ourselves into believing the old idea that we can get out when we are ready. Experience has proven this to be all untrue. Many have tried and many have failed. Some even believe this is a needed mindset. They are truly misinformed. Many have tried to counsel active gangsters with their directive based on cultural dignity. We must remember our mentality displays itself in all forms of separation, false pride in everything other than our higher power. This method continued to keep us angry and confused.

Encouragement from the court helps us to find relief we had so aggressively searched for. However we arrive we must smash the illusion Honesty has to replace denial before we can face the truth about our gangsters mentality. We are certain many can remember when the jig was up. We can remember when the excitement, popularity and prosperity ceased to work. Jails, institutions and death began to appear all around us. We could no longer justify our way of life.

For members of the G. A. Fellowship to truly recover we must practice complete honesty. When practicing this gangsters lifestyle dishonesty was our only solution. Admission to this factors the door and allows us to enter the land of the average person. We can set a goal of becoming above average because we have experienced horrors to learn from. No matter the outcome we must never quit trying to achieve a completely non gangster lifestyle. Learning how to live a Non gangster lifestyle is a continuing task. As our crime free days grow we continue to work the steps.

Listen, if you will, to these three statements. First, Gangsters Anonymous does not demand that you believe anything. All of its twelve steps are but suggestions. Second, to become crime free and to stay crime free, you don't have to swallow all of Step Two right now. Looking back, I find that I took it piecemeal myself. Third, all you really need is a truly open mind. Just resign from the debating society and quit bothering yourself with such deep questions as, whether it was the hen or the egg that came first. Again I say, all you need is the open mind."

The sponsor continues, "Take, for example, my own case. I had a Criminal Justice schooling. Naturally I respected, venerated, even worshiped crime and money.

As a matter of fact, I still want money. Time after time, my instructors held up to me the basic principle of all types of financial progress: search and research, again and again, always with the open mind. When I first looked at being a recovering gangster, my reaction was just like yours. This recovering gangster business, I thought, is totally uneconomical. This I can't swallow. I simply won't consider such nonsense.

"Then I woke up. I had to admit that recovering gangsters were showing results, prodigious results. I saw that my attitude regarding these people had been anything but scientific. It wasn't recovering gangsters that had the closed mind, it was me. The minute I stopped arguing, I could begin to see and feel. Right there, Step Two gently and very gradually began to infiltrate my life. I can't say upon what occasion or upon what day I came to believe in a power greater than myself, but I certainly have that belief now. To acquire it, I had only to stop fighting and practice the rest of the G.A. program as enthusiastically as I could.

"This is only one man's opinion based on his own experience, of course. I must quickly assure you that recovering gangsters tread innumerable paths in their quest for faith. If you don't care for the one I've suggested, you'll be sure to discover one that suits you if only you look and listen. Many men like us have begun to solve the problem by the method of substitution. You can, if you wish, make G.A. itself your 'higher power.' Here's a very large group of people who have solved their gangster's mentality problem. In this respect they are certainly a power greater than you, who have not even come close to a solution. Surely you can have faith in them. Even this minimum of faith will be enough. You will find many members who have crossed the threshold just this way. All of them will tell you that, once across, their faith broadened and deepened. Relieved of the gangster's mentality obsession, their life unaccountably transformed, they came to believe in a Higher Power, and most of them began to talk of God."

Consider next *the* plight of those who once had faith, but have lost it. There will be those who have drifted into indifference, those filled with self sufficiency who have cut themselves off, those who have become prejudiced against religion, and those who are downright defiant because God has failed to fulfill their demands. Can a single recovering gangster's experience tell all that they may still find a faith that works?

Sometimes recovery comes harder to those who have lost or rejected faith than to those who never had any faith at all, for they think they have tried faith and found it wanting. They have tried the way of faith and the way of no faith. Since both ways have proved bitterly disappointing, they have concluded there is no place whatsoever for them to go. The roadblocks of indifference, fancied self sufficiency, prejudice, and defiance often prove more solid and formidable for these people than any erected by the unconvinced agnostic or even the militant atheist. Religion says the existence of God can be proved; the agnostic says it *can't* be proved; and the atheist claims proof of the nonexistence of God. Obviously, the dilemma of the wanderer from faith is that of profound confusion. He thinks himself lost to the comfort of any conviction at all. He cannot attain even in a small degree the assurance of the believer, the agnostic, or the atheist. He is the bewildered one.

Any number of recovering gangsters can say to the drifter, "Yes, we were diverted from our childhood faith, too. The overconfidence of youth was too much for us. Of course, we were glad that good home and religious training had given us certain values. We were still sure that we ought to be fairly honest, tolerant, and just, that we ought to be ambitious and hardworking. We became convinced that such simple rules of fair play and decency would be enough.

"As material success founded upon no more than these ordinary attributes began to come to us, we felt we were winning at the game of life. This was exhilarating, and it made us happy. Why should we be bothered with theological abstractions and religious duties, or with the state of our souls here or hereafter? The here and now was good enough for us. The will to win would carry us through. But then the gangster's mentality began to have its way with us. Finally, when all our score cards read 'zero,' and we saw that one more strike would put us out of the game forever, we had to look for our lost faith. It was in recovery that we rediscovered it. And so can you."

Now we come to another kind of problem: the

intellectually self sufficient man or woman. To these, many recovering gangsters can say, "Yes, we were like you, far too smart for our own good. We loved to have people call us precocious. We used our education to blow ourselves up into prideful balloons, though we were careful to hide this from others. Secretly, we felt we could float above the rest of the folks on our brainpower alone. Scientific progress told us there was nothing man couldn't do. Knowledge was all powerful. Intellect could conquer nature. Since, we were brighter than most folks (so we thought), the spoils of victory would be ours for the taking. The god of intellect displaced the God of our fathers. But again Freeway Rick had other ideas. We who had won so handsomely in the gangster walk turned into all time losers. We saw that we had to reconsider or die. We found many in recovery who once thought as we did. They helped us to get down to our right size. By their example they showed us that humility and intellect could be compatible, provided we placed humility first. When we began to do that, we received the gift of faith, a faith which works. This faith is for you, too."

Another crowd of recovering gangsters might say: "We were plumb disgusted with religion and all its works. The Bible, we said, was full of nonsense; we could cite it chapter and verse, and we couldn't see the Beatitudes for the 'begets.' In spots its morality was impossibly good; in others it seemed impossibly bad. But it was the morality of the religionists themselves that really got us down. We gloated over the hypocrisy, bigotry, and crushing self righteousness that clung to so many 'believers' even in their Sunday best. How we loved to shout the damaging fact that millions of the 'good men of religion' were still killing one another off in the name of God. This all meant, of course, that we had substituted negative for positive thinking. After we came to G.A. , we had to recognize that this trait had been an ego feeding proposition. In belaboring the sins of some religious people, we could feel superior to all of them. More over, we could avoid looking at some of our own shortcomings. Self righteousness, the very thing that we had contemptuously condemned in others, was our own besetting evil. This phony form of respectability was our undoing, so far as faith was concerned. But finally, driven into recovery, we learned better.

"As psychiatrists have often observed, defiance is the outstanding characteristic of many a gangster. So it's not strange that lots of us have had our day at defying God Himself. Sometimes it's because God has not delivered us the good things of life which we specified, just as a greedy child often makes an impossible list for Santa Claus. More often, though, we had met up with some major calamity and, to our way of thinking lost out because God deserted us. The girl we wanted to marry had other notions; we prayed to God that she'd change her mind, but she didn't. We prayed for healthy children, and were presented with sick ones, or none at all. We prayed for promotions at work, and none came. Loved ones, upon whom we heartily depended, were taken from us by so called acts of God. Then we became gangsters, and asked God to stop that.

But nothing happened. This was the unkindest cut of all. 'Damn this faith business!' we said.

"When we encountered G.A., the fallacy of our defiance was revealed. At no time had we asked what God's will was for us; instead we had been telling Him what it ought to be. No man, we saw, could believe in God and defy Him, too. Belief meant reliance, not defiance. In recovery we saw the fruits of this belief: men and women spared from a criminal's final catastrophe. We saw them meet and transcend their other pains and trials. We saw them calmly accept impossible situations, seeking neither to run nor to recriminate. This was not only faith; it was faith that worked under all conditions. We soon concluded that whatever price in humility we must pay, we would pay." Now let's take the guy full of faith, but still committing crimes. He believes he is devout. His religious observance is scrupulous. He's sure he still believes in God, but suspects that God doesn't believe in him. He takes pledges and more pledges. Following each, he not only commits crimes again, but acts worse than the last time. Valiantly he tries to fight this criminal mentality, imploring God's help, but the help doesn't come. What, then, can be the matter?

To clergymen, doctors, friends, and families, the gangster who means well and tries hard is a heartbreaking riddle. To most recovering gangsters, he is not. There are too many of us who have been just like him, and have found the riddle's answer. This answer has to do with the quality of faith rather than its quantity. This has been our blind spot. We supposed we had humility when really we hadn't. We supposed we had been serious about religious practices when, upon honest appraisal, we found we had been only superficial. Or, going to the other extreme, we had wallowed in emotionalism and had mistaken it for true religious feeling. In both cases, we had been asking something for nothing. The fact was we really hadn't cleaned house so that the grace of God could enter us and expel the obsession. In no deep or meaningful sense had we ever taken stock of ourselves, made amends to those we had harmed, or freely given to any other human being without any demand for reward. We had not even prayed rightly. We had always said, "Grant me my wishes" instead of "Thy will be done." The love of God and man we understood not at all. Therefore, we remained self deceived, and so incapable of receiving enough grace to restore us to sanity.

Few indeed are the practicing gangsters who have any idea how irrational they are, or seeing their irrationality, can bear to face it. Some will be willing to term themselves "revolutionaries," but cannot endure the suggestion that they are in fact mentally ill. They are abetted in this blindness by a world which does not understand the similarity between committing crimes and a gangster mentality. "Sanity" is deemed as "soundness of mind." Yet no gangster, now crime free, and trying to analyze his destructive behavior, whether the destruction fell on the dining room furniture or his own moral fiber, can claim "soundness of mind" for himself.

Therefore, Step Two is the rallying point for all of us. Whether agnostic, atheist, or former believer, we can stand together on this Step. True humility and an open mind can lead us to faith, and every G.A. meeting is an assurance that God will restore us to sanity if we rightly relate ourselves to Him.

STEP THREE

"We made a decision to turn our will and our life over to the care of God as we understood Him".

As gangsters, we turned our will and our life over many times to a destructive power. Our will and our life were forbidden to fly by our destructive mentality. We looked for the instant gratification that the gangster life gave us. During that time, our total being body, mind and spirit – was under enemy control by this destructive mentality. For a time, it was pleasurable, then the euphoria began to wear off and we saw the ugly side of gangster living.

We found that the higher our gangster mentality

took us, the lower it brought us. We faced two choices: either we suffered the pain of rejection or deeper involvement. For all of us, the day came when there was no longer a choice; we had to live like a gangster. Having given our will and life to our gangster living, in utter desperation, we looked for another way. In Gangsters Anonymous, we decided to turn our will and our life over to the care of God, as we understand Him. This is a giant step. We do not have to be religious; anyone can take this step. All that is required is willingness. All that is essential is that we open the door to a Power greater than ourselves. Our concept of God comes not from dogma but from what we believe and from what works for us. Many of us understand God to be simply whatever force keeping us crime free. The right to a God of your understanding is total and without any catches. Because we have this right, it is necessary to be honest about our belief if we are to grow spiritually. We found that all we needed to do was try. When we gave our best effort, the program worked for us as it has worked for countless others. The Third Step does not say, "We turned our will and our life over to the care of God. It says, "We made a decision to rum our will and our life over to the care of God as we understood Him." We made the decision, no one, our friends, families, a probation officer, judge, therapist or doctor did not make it for us. We made it! For the first time since that first gangster thought, we have made a decision for ourselves. The word "decision" implies action. Our decision is faith. We have only to believe that the miracle we see working in the life of those who are crime free can happen to any gangster with the desire to change. We simply realize there is a force for spiritual growth that can help us become more tolerant, patient, and useful in helping others. Many of us have said, "Take my will and my life. Guide me in my recovery. Show me how to live."

The relief of "letting go and letting God" helps us develop a life that is worth living. Surrendering to the will of our Higher Power gets easier with daily practice. When we honestly try, it works. Many of us start our day with a simple request for guidance from our Higher Power. Although we know that "turning it over" works, we may still take our will and life back. We may even get angry because God permits it. At times during our recovery, the decision to ask for God's help is our greatest source of strength and courage. We cannot make this decision often enough. We surrender quietly, and let the God of our understanding take care of us. At first, our heads reeled with the questions: "What will happen when I turn my life over? Will I become 'perfect'?" We may have been more realistic than this. Some of us had to turn to an experienced G.A. member and ask, "What was it like for you?" The answer will vary from member to member. Most of us feel that open-mindedness, willingness and surrender are the keys to this step. We have surrendered our will and our life to the care of a Power greater than ourselves.

If we are thorough and sincere, we will notice a change for the better. Our fears narrow, and faith begins to grow as we learn the true meaning of surrender. We are no longer fighting fear, anger, guilt, self-pity or depression. We realize that the Power that brought us to this program is still with us and will continue to guide us if we allow it. We are slowly beginning to lose the paralyzing fear of hopelessness. The proof of this step is in the way we live. We have come to enjoy living crime free and want more of the good things that the G.A. Fellowship holds for us. We know now that we cannot pause in our spiritual program; we want all that we can get. We are now ready for our first honest self-appraisal, and we begin with Step Four. Practicing Step Three is like the opening of a door which to all appearances is still closed and locked. All we need is a key, and the decision to swing the door open. There is only one key, and it is called willingness. Once unlocked by willingness, the door opens almost of itself, and looking through it, we shall see a pathway beside which is an inscription. It reads: "This is the way to a faith that works." In the first two Steps we were engaged in reflection. We saw that we were powerless over our gangsters' mentality, but we also perceived that faith of some kind, if only in recovery itself, is possible to anyone. These conclusions did not require action; they required only acceptance.

Like all the remaining Steps, Step Three calls for affirmative action, for it is only by action that we can cut away the self will which has always blocked the entry of God or, if you like, a Higher Power into our life. Faith, to be sure, is necessary, but faith alone can avail nothing. We can have faith, yet keep God out of our life. Therefore our problem now becomes just how and by what specific means shall we be able to let Him in? Step Three represents our first attempt to do this. In fact, the effectiveness of the whole G.A. program will rest upon how well and earnestly we have tried to come to "a decision to turn our will and our life over to the care of God *as we understood Him.*" To every worldly and practical minded beginner, this Step looks hard, even impossible. No matter how much one wishes to try, exactly how *can* he turn his own will and his own life over to the care of whatever God he thinks there is? Fortunately, we who have tried it, with equal misgivings, can testify that anyone, anyone at all, can begin to do it. We can further add that a beginning, even the smallest one, is all that is needed. Once we have placed the key of willingness in the lock and have the door ever so slightly opened, we find that we can always open it some more. Though self will may slam it shut again, as it frequently does, it will always respond the moment we again pick up the key of willingness.

Maybe this all sounds mysterious and remote, something like Einstein's theory of relativity or a proposition in nuclear physics. It isn't at all. Let's look at how practical it actually is. Every man and woman who has joined us in recovery from this criminal behavior and intends to stick with it has, without realizing it, made a beginning on Step Three. Isn't it true that in all matters touching upon a gangster's mentality, each one of them has decided to turn his or her life over to the care, protection, and guidance of Gangsters Anonymous? Already a willingness has been achieved to cast out one's own will and one's own ideas about the criminal mentality problem in favor of those suggested by recovering gangsters. Any willing newcomer feels sure recovery is the only safe harbor for the floundering vessel he has become. Now if this is not turning one's will and life over to a newfound providence, then what is it? But suppose that instinct still cries out, as it certainly will, "Yes, respecting a gangster's mentality, I guess I have to be dependent upon recovery, but in all other matters I must still maintain my independence. Nothing is going to turn me into a non entity. If I keep on turning my life and my will over to the care of something or somebody else, what will be come of *me.* I'll look like the hole in the doughnut." This, of course, is the process by which instinct and logic always seek to bolster egotism, and so frustrate spiritual development. The trouble is that this kind of thinking takes no real account of the facts. And the facts seem to be these: The more we become willing to depend upon a Higher Power, the more independent we actually are. Therefore dependence, as G.A. practices it, is really a means of gaining true independence of the spirit.

Let's examine for a moment this idea of dependence at the level of everyday living. In this area it is startling to discover how dependent we really are, and how unconscious we are of that dependence. Every modern house has electric wiring carrying power and light to its interior. We are delighted with this dependence; our main hope is that nothing will ever cut off the supply of current. By so accepting our dependence upon this marvel of science, we find ourselves more independent personally. Not only are we more independent, we are even more comfortable and secure. Power flows just where it is needed. Silently and surely, electricity, that strange energy so few people understand, meets our simplest daily needs, and our most desperate ones, too. Ask the polio sufferer confined to an iron lung who depends with complete trust upon a motor to keep the breath of life in him.

But the moment our mental or emotional independence is in question, how differently we behave. How persistently we claim the right to decide all by ourselves just what we shall think and just how we shall act. Oh yes, we'll weigh the pros and cons of every problem. We'll listen politely to those who would advise us, but all the decisions are to be ours alone. Nobody is going to meddle with our personal independence in such matters. Besides, we think, there is no one we can surely trust. We are certain that our intelligence, backed by willpower, can rightly control our inner life and guarantee us success in the world we live in. This brave philosophy, wherein each man plays God, sounds good in the speaking, but it still has to meet the acid test: how well does it actually work? One good look in the mirror ought to be answer enough for any gangster.

Should his own image in the mirror be too awful to contemplate (and it usually is), he might first take a look at the results normal people are getting from self sufficiency. Everywhere he sees people filled with anger and fear, society breaking up into warring fragments. Each fragment says to the other, "We are right and you are wrong." Every such pressure group, if it is strong enough, self righteously imposes its will upon the rest. And everywhere the same thing is being done on an individual basis. The sum of all this mighty effort is less peace and less brotherhood than before. The philosophy of self sufficiency is not paying off. Plainly enough, it is a bone crushing juggernaut whose final achievement is ruin.

Therefore, we who are gangsters can consider ourselves fortunate indeed. Each of us has had his own near fatal encounter with the juggernaut of self will, and has suffered enough under its weight to be willing to look for something better. So it is by circumstance rather than by any virtue that we have been driven to recovery, have admitted defeat, have acquired the rudiments of faith, and now want to make a decision to turn our will and our life over to a Higher Power.

We realize that the word "dependence" is as distasteful to many psychiatrists and psychologists as it is to gangsters. Like our professional friends, we, too, are aware that there are wrong forms of dependence. We have experienced many of them. No adult man or woman, for example, should be in too much emotional dependence upon a parent. They should have been weaned long before, and if they have not been, they should wake up to that fact. This very form of faulty dependence has caused many a rebellious gangster mentality to conclude that dependence of any sort must be intolerably damaging. But dependence upon an recovering gangster group or upon a Higher Power hasn't produced any baleful results.

When the Iraq War broke out, this spiritual principle had its first major test, recovering gangsters entered the services and were scattered all over the world. Would they be able to take discipline, stand up under fire, and endure the monotony and misery of war? Would the kind of dependence they had learned in recovery carry them through? Well, it did. They had even fewer criminal lapses or emotional binges than recovering gangsters safe at home did. They were just as capable of endurance and valor as any other soldiers. Whether in Alaska or on the Salerno beachhead, their dependence upon a Higher Power worked. And far from being a weakness, this dependence was their chief source of strength. So how, exactly, can the willing person continue to turn his will and his life over to the Higher Power? He made a beginning, we have seen, when he commenced to rely upon G.A. for the solution of his gangster's mentality problem.

By now, though, the chances are that he has become convinced that he has more problems than just a gangster's mentality, and that some of these need to be solved by all the sheer personal determination and courage he can muster. They simply will not budge; they make him desperately unhappy and threaten his new crime free life. Our friend is still victimized by remorse when he thinks of yesterday. Bitterness still overpowers when he broods upon those he still envies or hates, financial insecurity worries him sick, and panic takes over when he thinks of all the bridges to safety that his gangster's mentality has burned.

And how shall he ever straighten out an awful jam that cost him the affection of his family and separated him from them? His lone courage and unflinching will cannot do it. Surely, he must now depend upon somebody or something else.

At first that "somebody" is likely to be his closest recovering gangster. He relies upon the assurance that his many troubles, made more acute because he cannot use the gangster's mentality to kill the pain, can be solved, too. Of course, the sponsor points out that our friend's life is still unmanageable even though he is crime free, that after all, is only a bare start after a recovering gangster's pro has been made. More crime free living brought about by the admission of a gangster mentality and by attendance at a few meetings is very good indeed, but it is bound to be a far cry from permanent crime free living and a contented, useful life. That is just where the remaining Steps of the recovering gangster program come in. Nothing short of continuous action upon these steps as a way of life can bring the much desired result.

Then, it is explained that other Steps of the recovering gangster program can be practiced with success only when Step Three is given a determined and persistent trial. This statement may surprise newcomers who have experienced nothing but constant deflation and a growing conviction that human will is of no value whatever. They have become persuaded, and rightly so, that their many problems, in addition to a gangsters' mentality, will not yield to a headlong assault powered by the individual alone. But now it appears that there are certain things which only the individual can do. All by himself, and in the light of his own circumstances, he needs to develop the quality of willingness. When he acquires willingness, he is the only one who can make the decision to exert himself. Trying to do this is an act of his own will. All of the Twelve Steps require sustained and personal exertion to conform to their principles and so, we trust, to God's will.

It is when we try to make our will conform with God's that we begin to use it rightly. To all of us, this was a most wonderful revelation. *Our troubles had been the misuse of willpower. We tried to bombard our problems with it instead of attempting to bring it into agreement with God's intention for us.* To make this increasingly possible is the purpose of the recovering gangsters' Twelve Steps, and Step Three opens the door.

Once we have come into agreement with these ideas, it is really easy to begin the practice of Step Three. In all times of emotional disturbance or indecision, we can pause, ask for quiet, and in the stillness simply say: "God grant me the serenity to accept the things I cannot change, courage to change the things I can, and wisdom to know the difference. Thy will, not mine, be done."

STEP FOUR

"We made a searching and fearless moral inventory of ourselves."

The purpose of a searching and fearless moral inventory is to sort through the confusion and the contradiction of our life, so that we can find out who we really are. We are starting a new way of life and need to be clear of the burdens and traps that controlled us and prevented our growth. As we approach this step, most of us are afraid that there is a monster inside of us that, if released, will destroy us. This fear can cause us to put off our inventory or may even prevent us from taking this crucial step at all. We have found that fear is a lack of faith, and we have found a loving, personal God to whom we can turn. We no longer need to be afraid we have been experts at self-deception and rationalization. By writing our inventory, we can overcome these obstacles. A written inventory will unlock parts of our subconscious that remain hidden when we simply think about or talk about who we are. Once it is all down on paper, it is much easier to see, and much harder to deny our true nature.

Honest self-assessment is one of the keys to our new way of life. Let us face it; when we were living life gangster style, we were not honest with ourselves. We are becoming honest with ourselves when we admit that gangster living has defeated us and that we need help. It took a long time to admit that we were beaten. We found that we do not recover physically, mentally or spiritually overnight.

Step Four will help us toward our recovery. Most of us were neither as terrible, nor as wonderful, as we supposed. We are surprised to find that we have good points in our inventory. Anyone who has worked this step will tell you that the Fourth Step was a turning point in his or her life. Some of us make the mistake of approaching the Fourth Step as if it were a confession of how horrible we are what a bad person we have been. In this new way of life, a binge of emotional sorrow can be dangerous. This is not the purpose of the Fourth Step. We are trying to free ourselves of living in old, useless patterns. We take the Fourth Step to grow and to gain strength and insight. We may approach the Fourth Step in a number of ways.

To have the faith and courage to write a fearless inventory, Steps One, Two and Three are the necessary preparation. It is advisable that before we start, we go over the first three steps with a sponsor. We get comfortable with our understanding of these steps. We allow ourselves the privilege of feeling good about what we are doing. We have been thrashing about for a long time and have gotten nowhere. Now we start the Fourth Step and let go of fear.

We simply put it on paper, to the best of our present ability.

We must be done with the past, not cling to it. We want to look our past in the face, see it for what it really was and release it so we can live today. The past, for most of us, has been a ghost in the closet. We have been afraid to open that closet for fear of what that ghost may do to us. We do not have to look at the past alone. Our wills and our life are now in the hands of our Higher Power. Step Four will help us toward our recovery. Most of us were neither as terrible, nor as wonderful, as we supposed. We are surprised to find that we have good points in our inventory. Anyone who has some time in the program and has worked this step will tell you that the Fourth Step was a turning point in his or her life. Some of us make the mistake of approaching the Fourth Step as if it were a confession of how horrible we are–what a bad person we have been. In this new way of life, a binge of emotional sorrow can be dangerous. This is not the purpose of the Fourth Step. We are trying to free ourselves of living in old, useless patterns.

We take the Fourth Step to grow and to gain strength and insight. We may approach the Fourth Step in a number of ways. To have the faith and courage to write a fearless inventory, Steps One, Two and Three are the necessary preparation.

It is advisable before we start, we go over the first three steps with a sponsor. We get comfortable with our understanding of these steps. We allow ourselves the privilege of feeling good about what we are doing. We have been thrashing about for a long time and have gotten nowhere. Now we start the Fourth Step and let go of fear. We simply put it on paper, to the best of our present ability. We must be done with the past, not cling to it. We want to look our past in the face, see it for what it really was and release it so we can live today. The past, for most of us, has been a ghost in the closet. We have been afraid to open that closet for fear of what that ghost may do to us. We do not have to look at the past alone. Our wills and our life are now in the hands of our Higher Power. Writing a thorough and honest inventory seemed impossible. It was, as long as we were operating under our own power. We take a few quiet moments before writing and ask for the strength to be fearless and thorough.

In Step Four, we begin to get in touch with ourselves. We write about our liabilities such as guilt, shame, remorse, self-pity, resentment, anger, depression, frustration, confusion, loneliness, anxiety, betrayal, hopelessness, failure, fear and denial. We write about the things that bother us here and now. We have a tendency to think negatively, so putting it on paper gives us a chance to look more positively at what is happening. Assets must also be considered, if we are to get an accurate and complete picture of ourselves. This is very difficult for most of us, because it is hard to accept that we have good qualities. However, we all have assets, many of them newly found in the program, such as being crime free, open-mindedness, God-awareness, honesty with others, acceptance, positive action, sharing, willingness, courage, faith, caring, gratitude, kindness and generosity. In addition, our inventories usually include material on relationships. We review our past performance and our present behavior to see what we want to keep and what we want to discard. No one is forcing us to give up our misery. This step has the reputation of being difficult; in reality, it is quite simple. We write our inventory without considering the Fifth Step. We work Step Four as if there were no Step Five. We can write alone or near other people; whatever is more comfortable to the writer is fine. We can write as long or as short as needed. Someone with experience can help. The important thing is to write a moral inventory. If the word "moral" bothers us, we may call it a positive/negative inventory.

The way to write an inventory is to write it! Thinking about an inventory, talking about it, theorizing about the inventory will not get it written. We sit down with a notebook, ask for guidance, pick up our pen and start writing. Anything we think about is inventory material. When we realize how little we have to lose, and how much we have to gain, we begin this step. A basic rule of thumb is that we can write too little, yet we can never write too much. The inventory will fit the individual. Perhaps this seems difficult or painful. It may appear impossible. We may fear that being in touch with our feelings will trigger an overwhelming chain reaction of pain and panic. We may feel like avoiding an inventory because of a fear of failure.

When we ignore our feelings, the tension becomes too much for us. The fear of impending doom is so great that it overrides our fear of failure. An inventory becomes a relief, because the pain of doing it is less than the pain of not doing it. We learn that pain can be a motivating factor in recovery. Thus, facing it becomes unavoidable. Every topic of step meetings seems to be on the Fourth Step or doing a daily inventory. Through the inventory process, we are able to deal with all the things that can build up. The more we live our program, the more God seems to put us in positions where issues surface. When issues surface, we write about them.

We begin enjoying our recovery because we have a way to resolve shame, guilt, or resentment. The stress is imprisoned. Writing will lift the lid off our pressure cooker. We decide whether we want to serve it up, put the lid back on it, or throw it out. We no longer have to stew in it. We sit down with paper and pen and ask for our God's help in revealing the defects that are causing our pain and suffering. We pray for the courage to be fearless and thorough and that this inventory may help us to put our life in order. When we pray and take action, it always goes better for us. We are not going to be perfect. If we were perfect, we would not be human. The important thing is that we do our best. We use the tools available to us, and we develop the ability to survive our emotions. We do not want to lose any of what we have gained; we want to continue in the program. It is our experience that no matter how searching and thorough, no inventory is of any lasting effect unless an equally thorough Fifth Step promptly follows it. Creation gave us instincts for a purpose. Without them we wouldn't be complete human beings. If men and women didn't exert themselves to be secure in their persons, made no effort to harvest food or construct shelter, there would be no survival. If they didn't reproduce, the earth wouldn't be populated. If there were no social instinct, if men cared nothing for the society of one another, there would be no society. Desires for sex relations, for material and emotional security, and for companionship are perfectly necessary and right, and surely God given.

Yet these instincts, so necessary for our existence, often far exceed their proper functions. Powerfully, blindly, many times subtly, they drive us, dominate us, and insist upon ruling our life. Our desires for sex, for material and emotional security, and for an important place in society often tyrannize us. Thus when out of joint, man's natural desires cause him great trouble, practically all the trouble there is. No human being, however good, is exempt from these troubles. Nearly every serious emotional problem can be seen as a case of misdirected instinct. When that happens, our great natural assets, our instincts, have turned into physical and mental liabilities.

Step Four is our vigorous and painstaking effort to discover what these liabilities in each of us have been, and are. We want to find exactly how, when, and where our natural desires have warped us. We wish to look squarely at the unhappiness this has caused others and ourselves. By discovering what our emotional deformities are, we can move toward their correction. Without a willing and persistent effort, to do this, there can be little crime free living or contentment for us. Without a searching and fearless moral inventory, most of us have found that the faith which really works in daily living is still out of reach.

Before tackling the inventory problem in detail, let's have a closer look at what the basic problem is. Simple examples like the following take on a world of meaning when we think about them. Suppose a person places sexual desires ahead of everything else. In such a case, this imperious urge can destroy his chances for material and emotional security as well as his standing in the community. Another may develop such as an obsession for financial security that he wants to do nothing but hoard money. Going to the extreme, he can become a miser, or even a recluse who denies himself both family and friends.

Nor is the quest for security always expressed in terms of money. How frequently we see a frightened human being determined to depend completely upon a stronger person for guidance and protection. This weak one, failing to meet life's responsibilities with his own resources, never grows up. Disillusionment and helplessness are his lot. In time all his protectors either flee or die, and he is once more left alone and afraid. We have also seen men and women who go power mad, who devote themselves to attempting to rule their fellow man. These people often throw to the winds every chance for legitimate security and a happy family life. Whenever a human being becomes a battleground for the instincts, there can be no peace.

But that is not all of the danger. Every time a person imposes his instincts unreasonably upon others, unhappiness follows. If the pursuit of wealth tramples upon people who happen to be in the way, then anger, jealousy, and revenge are likely to be aroused. If sex runs riot, there is a similar uproar. Demands made upon other people for too much attention, protection, and love can only invite domination or revulsion in the protectors themselves which are two emotions quite as unhealthy as the demands which evoked them. When an individual's desire for prestige becomes uncontrollable, whether in the sewing circle or at the international conference table, other people suffer and often revolt. This collision of instincts can produce anything from a cold snub to a blazing revolution. In these ways we are set in conflict not only with ourselves, but with other people who have instincts, too.

Recovering gangsters should be able to see that instinct run wild in them and that is the underlying cause of their destructive criminal behavior. We began our life of crime to drown feelings of fear, frustration, and depression. We broke laws to escape the guilt of our passions, and then broke laws again to make more passions possible. We joined gangs and active criminal groups for vain glory that we might enjoy foolish dreams of pomp and power. This perverse soul sickness is not pleasant to look upon. Instincts on rampage balk at investigation. The minute we make a serious attempt to probe them, we are liable to suffer severe reactions.

Temporarily we are on the depressive side and we are apt to be swamped with guilt and self loathing. We enjoy this messy bog, often getting misshapen and painful pleasure out of it. As we morbidly pursue this melancholy activity, we may sink to such a point of despair that nothing but oblivion looks possible as a solution. Here, of course, we have lost all perspective, and therefore all genuine humility. For this is pride in reverse. This is not a moral inventory at all; it is the very process by which the depressive has so often been led to criminal behavior and extinction.

If, however, our natural disposition is inclined to self righteousness or grandiosity, our reaction will be just the opposite. We will be offended by G. A.'s suggested inventory. No doubt we shall point with pride to the good life we thought we led before crime cut us down. We shall claim that our serious character defects, if we think we have any at all, have been caused chiefly by society's ills or excessive crimes. This being so, we think it logically follows that crime free first, last, and all the time is the only thing we need to work for. We believe that our characters will be revived the moment we quit living criminally. If we were nice people all along, except for our sometimes criminal behavior, what need is there for a moral inventory, now that we are crime free?

We also clutch at another wonderful excuse for

avoiding an inventory. Our present anxieties and troubles, we cry, are caused by the behavior of other people and people who really need a moral inventory. We firmly believe that if only they'd treat us better, we'd be all right. Therefore, we think our indignation is justified and reasonable that our resentments are the "right kind." *We* aren't the guilty ones. *They* are! At this stage of the inventory proceedings, our sponsors come to the rescue. They can do this, for they are the carriers of G.A's tested experience with Step Four. They comfort the melancholy one by first showing him that his case is not strange or different, that his character defects are probably not more numerous or worse than those of anyone else in recovery. This the sponsor promptly proves by talking freely and easily, and without exhibitionism, about his own defects, past and present. This calm, yet realistic, stock taking is immensely reassuring. The sponsor probably points out that the newcomer has some assets which can be noted along with his liabilities. This tends to clear away morbidity and encourage balance. As soon as he begins to be more objective, the newcomer can fearlessly, rather than fearfully, look at his own defects.

The sponsors of those who feel they need no inventory are confronted with quite another problem. This is because people who are driven by pride of self unconsciously blind themselves to their liabilities. These newcomers scarcely need comforting. The problem is to help them discover a chink in the walls their ego has built, through which the light of reason can shine.

First off, they can be told that the majority of recovering gangsters have suffered severely from self justification during their crime days. For most of us, self justification was the maker of excuses; excuses, of course, for committing crimes, and for all kinds of crazy and damaging conduct. We had made the invention of alibis a fine art. We had to commit crimes because times were hard or times were good. We had to commit crimes because at home we were smothered with love or got none at all. We had to commit crimes because at work we were great successes or dismal failures. We had to commit crimes because our nation had won a war or lost at peace. And so it goes, ad infinitum.

We thought "conditions" drove us to commit crimes, and when we tried to correct these conditions and found that we couldn't **to** our entire satisfaction, our committing crimes went out of hand and we became gangsters/criminals. It never occurred to us that we needed to change ourselves to meet the conditions, whatever they were. But in recovery, we slowly learned that something had to be done about our vengeful resentments, self pity, and unwarranted pride. We had to see that every time we played the big shot, we turned people against us. We had to see that when we harbored grudges and planned revenge for such defeats, we were really beating ourselves with the club of anger we had intended to use on others. We learned that if we were seriously disturbed, our *first* need was to quiet that disturbance, regardless of who or what we thought caused it. To see how erratic emotions victimized us often takes a long time. We could perceive them quickly in others, but only slowly in ourselves. First of all, we had to admit that we had many of these defects, even though such disclosures were painful and humiliating. Where other people were concerned, we had to drop the word "blame" from our speech and thought. This required great willingness even to begin Step Five. Once over the first two or three high hurdles, the course ahead began to look easier. We started to get perspective on ourselves, which is another way of saying that we were gaining in humility.

Of course the depressive and the power driver are personality extremes, types with which recovering gangsters, and the whole world abound. Often these personalities are just as sharply defined as the examples given. But just as often some of us will fit more or less into both classifications. Human beings are never quite alike, so each of us, when making an inventory, will need to determine what his individual character defects are. Having found the shoes that fit, he ought to step into them and walk with new confidence that he is at last on the right track.

Now let's ponder the need for a list of the more glaring personality defects all of us have in varying degrees. To those having religious training, such a list would set forth serious violations of moral principles. Some others will think of this list as defects of character. Still others will call it an index of maladjustment's. Some will become quite annoyed if there is talk about immorality, let alone sin. But all who are remotely reasonable will agree upon one point: that there is plenty wrong with us gangsters about which plenty will have to be done if we are to expect crime free living, progress, and any real ability to cope with life.

To avoid falling into confusion over the names these defects should be called, let's take a universally recognized list of major human failings, the Seven Deadly Sins of pride, greed, lust, anger, gluttony, envy, and sloth. It is not by accident that pride heads the procession. For pride, leading to self justification, and always spurred by conscious or unconscious fears, is the basic breeder of most human difficulties, the chief block to true progress. Pride lures us into making demands upon ourselves or upon others which can not be met without perverting or misusing our God given instincts. When the satisfaction of our instincts for sex, security, and society becomes the sole object of our life, then pride steps in to justify our excesses.

All these failings generate fear, a soul sickness in its own right. Then fear, in turn, generates more character defects. Unreasonable fear that our instincts will not be satisfied drives us to covet the possessions of others, to lust for sex and power, to become angry when our instinctive demands are threatened, to be envious when the ambitions of others seem to be realized while ours are not. We eat, commit crimes, and grab for more of everything than we need, fearing we shall never have enough. And with genuine alarm at the prospect of work, we stay lazy. We loaf and procrastinate, or at best work grudgingly and under half steam. These fears are the termites that ceaselessly devour the foundation of whatever sort of life we try to build.

So when recovering gangsters suggest a fearless moral inventory, it seems to every newcomer that more is being asked of him than what he can do. Both his pride and his fear beat him back every time he tries to look within himself. Pride says, "You need not pass this way," and Fear says, "You dare not look!" But the testimony of recovering gangsters who have really tried a moral inventory is that pride and fear of this sort often turns out to be the bogeymen, nothing else. Once we have a complete willingness to take the inventory, and exert ourselves to do the job thoroughly, a wonderful light falls upon this foggy scene. As we persist, a brand new kind of confidence is born, and the sense of relief at finally facing ourselves is indescribable. These are the first fruits of Step Four.

By now the newcomer has probably arrived at the following conclusions: that his character defects, representing instincts gone astray, have been the primary cause of his committing crimes and his failure at life; that unless he is now willing to work hard at the elimination of the worst of these defects, both crime free living and peace of mind will still elude him; that all the faulty foundation of his life will have to be torn out and built anew on bedrock. Now, willing to commence the search for his own defects, he will ask, "Just how do I go about this? *How* do I take inventory of myself?"

Since Step Four is but the beginning of a lifetime practice, it can be suggested that he first have a look at those personal flaws which are acutely troublesome and fairly obvious. Using his best judgment of what has been right and what has been wrong, he might make a rough survey of his conduct with respect to his primary instincts for sex, security, and society. Looking back over his life, he can readily get underway by consideration of questions such as these:

When, and how, and in just what instances did my selfish pursuit of the sexual relation damage other people and me? What people were hurt, and how badly? Did I spoil my marriage and injure my children? Did I jeopardize my standing in the community? Just how did I react to these situations at the time? Did I burn with a guilt that nothing could extinguish? Or did I insist that I was the pursued and not the pursuer, and thus absolved myself? How have I reacted to frustration in sexual matters? When denied, did I become vengeful or depressed? Did I take it out on other people? If there was rejection or coldness at home, did I use this as a reason for promiscuity?

Also of importance for most gangsters are the questions they must ask about their behavior respecting financial and emotional security. In these areas fear, greed, possessiveness, and pride have too often done their worst. Surveying his business or employment record, almost any gangster can ask questions like these: In addition to my committing crimes problem, what character defects contributed to my financial instability? Did fear and inferiority about my fitness for my job destroy my confidence and fill me with conflict? Did I try to cover up those feelings of inadequacy by bluffing, cheating, lying, or evading responsibility or by complaining that others failed to recognize my truly exceptional abilities? Did I overvalue myself and play the big shot? Did I have such unprincipled ambition that I double crossed and undercut my associates? Was I extravagant? Did I recklessly borrow money, caring little whether it was repaid or not? Was I a penny pincher, refusing to support my family properly? Did I cut corners financially? What about the "quick money" deals, the credit card scams, and the con artist moves?

Businesswomen in G.A. will naturally find that many of these questions apply to them, too. But the female gangster in the house can also make the family financially insecure. She can joggle charge accounts, manipulate the food budget, spend her afternoons prostituting, and run her husband reputations into debt by her irresponsibility, waste, and extravagance. But all gangsters who have committed crimes and found themselves out of jobs, family, and friends will need to cross examine themselves ruthlessly to determine how their own personality defects have thus demolished their security.

The most common symptoms of emotional insecurity are worry, anger, self pity, and depression. These stem from causes which sometimes seem to be within us, and at other times to come from without. To take inventory in this respect we ought to consider carefully all personal relationships which bring continuous or recurring trouble.

It should be remembered that this kind of insecurity may arise in any area where instincts are threatened. Questioning directed to this end might run like this: Looking at both the past and present, what sexual situations have caused me anxiety, bitterness, frustration, or depression? Appraising each situation fairly, can I see where I have been at fault? Did these perplexities beset me because of selfishness or unreasonable demands? Or, if my disturbance was seemingly caused by the behavior of others, why do I lack the ability to accept conditions I cannot change? These are the sort of fundamental inquiries that can disclose the source of my discomfort and indicate whether I may be able to alter my own conduct and so adjust myself serenely to self discipline.

Suppose that financial insecurity constantly arouses these same feelings. I can ask myself: to what extent have my own mistakes fed my gnawing anxieties. And if the actions of others are part of the cause, what can I do about that? If I am unable to change the present state of affairs, am I willing to take the measures necessary to shape my life to conditions as they are? Questions like these, more of which will come to mind easily in each individual case, will help turn up the root causes.

But it is from our twisted relations with family, friends, and society at large that many of us have suffered the most. We have been especially stupid and stubborn about them. The primary fact that we fail to recognize is our total inability to form a true partnership with another human being. Our egomania digs two disastrous pitfalls. Either we insist upon dominating the people we know, or we depend upon them far too much. If we lean too heavily on people, they will sooner or later fail us, for they are human, too, and can not possibly meet our incessant demands. In this way our insecurity grows and festers. When we habitually try to manipulate others to our own willful desires, they revolt, and resist us heavily. Then we develop hurt feelings, a sense of persecution, and a desire to retaliate. As we redouble our efforts at control, and continue to fail, our suffering becomes acute and constant. We have not once sought to be one in a family, to be a friend among friends, to be a worker among workers, to be a useful member of society. Always we tried to struggle to the top of the heap, or to hide underneath it. This self centered behavior blocked a partnership relation with any one of those around us. Of true brotherhood we had small comprehension.

Some will object to many of the questions posed, because they think their own character defects have not been so glaring. To these it can be suggested that a conscientious examination is likely to reveal the very defects the objectionable questions are concerned with. Because our surface record hasn't looked too bad, we have frequently been abashed to find that this is so simply because we have buried these defects deep down in us under thick layers of self justification. Whatever the defects, they finally ambushed us into a gangsters mentality and misery. Therefore, thoroughness ought to be the watch word when taking inventory. In this connection, it is wise to write out our questions and answers. It will be an aid to clear thinking and honest appraisal. It will be the first tangible evidence of our complete willingness to move forward.

Step Five

"We admitted to God, to ourselves, and to another human being the exact nature of our wrongs."

The Fifth Step is the key to freedom. It allows us to live crime free in the present. Sharing the exact nature of our wrongs sets us free to live. After taking a thorough Fourth Step, we deal with the contents of our inventory. We know that if we keep these defects inside us, they will lead us back to this criminal mentality. Holding on to our past would eventually sicken us and keep us from taking part in our new way of life. If we are not honest when we take a Fifth Step, we will have the same negative results that dishonesty brought us in the past. Step Five suggests that we admit to God, to ourselves, and to another human being the exact nature of our wrongs. We looked at our wrongs, examined our behavior patterns, and started to see the deeper aspects of our illness. Now we sit with another person and share our inventory aloud. Our Higher Power will be with us during our Fifth Step. We will receive help and be free to face ourselves and another human being. It seemed unnecessary to admit the exact nature of our wrongs to our Higher Power. "God already knows that stuff," we rationalized. Although He already knows, the admission must come from our own lips to be truly effective.

Step Five is not simply a reading of Step Four. For years, we avoided seeing ourselves as we really were. We were ashamed of ourselves and felt isolated from the rest of the world. Now that we have the shameful part of our past trapped, we can sweep it out of our life if we face and admit it. It would be tragic to write it all down and then shove it in a drawer. These defects grow when we easily deny they are there, and die in exceptance of the hurt they have caused. Before coming to Gangsters Anonymous, we felt that no one could understand the things we had done. We feared that if we ever revealed ourselves as we were our strength would fade. One major reality for us is the total lack of support from some who have a financial risk in our growth as a fellowship.

Many gangsters are uncomfortable about this. We recognize that we have been realistic in feeling this way. Our fellow members do understand this. As we were explaining we must carefully choose the person who is to hear our Fifth Step; we must make sure that they know what we are doing and why we are doing it. Although there is no hard rule about the person of our choice, it is important that we trust the person. Only complete confidence in the person's integrity and discretion can make us willing to be thorough in this step. Some of us take our Fifth Step with a total stranger, although some of us feel more comfortable choosing a member of Gangsters Anonymous. We know that another gangster would be less likely to judge us with malice or misunderstanding. Once we make a choice and are actually alone with that person, we proceed with their encouragement. We want to be definite, honest and thorough, realizing that this is a life and death matter. Some of us tried to hide part of our past in an attempt to find an easier way of dealing with our inner feelings. We may think that we have done enough by writing about our past. We cannot afford this mistake. This step will expose our motives and our actions. We cannot expect these things to reveal them. Our embarrassment is eventually beat, and we can avoid future guilt. We do not procrastinate. We must be exact. We want to tell the truth, cut and dried, as quickly as possible. There is always a danger that we will exaggerate our wrongs. It is equally dangerous to minimize or rationalize our part in past situations. After all, we still want to sound good. Gangsters tend to live secret life. For many years, we covered low self-esteem by hiding behind phony images that we hoped would fool people. Unfortunately, we fooled ourselves more than anyone else.

Although we often appeared attractive and confident on the outside, we were really hiding a shaky, insecure person on the inside. Then there are some of us who are just totally confidant and wise to the point of fearless suicide. The masks have to go. We share our inventory in black and white, skipping nothing. We continue to approach this step with honesty and thoroughness until we finish. It is a great relief to get rid of all our secrets and to share the burden of our past. Usually, as we share this step, the listener will share some of his or her story too. We find that we are not unique. We see, by the acceptance of our confidant, that we can be time-honored the way we are. We may never be able to remember all of our past mistakes. We give it our best and most complete effort. We begin to experience real personal feelings of a spiritual nature. We had spiritual theories; we now begin to awaken to spiritual reality.

This initial examination of ourselves usually reveals some behavior patterns that we do not particularly like. However, facing these patterns and bringing them out in the open makes it possible for us to deal with them constructively. We cannot make these changes alone. We will need the help of God, as we understand Him, and the Fellowship of Gangsters Anonymous. The G.A. Twelve Steps asks us to go contrary to our natural desires . . . they all deflate our egos. When it comes to ego deflation, few Steps are harder to take than Five. But scarcely any Step is more necessary to longtime crime free living and peace of mind than this one to a recovering gangster. Experience has taught us we cannot live alone with our pressing problems and the character defects which cause **or** aggravate them. If we have swept the searchlight of Step Four back and forth over our careers, and it has revealed in stark relief those experiences we'd rather not remember, if we have come to know how wrong thinking and action have hurt us and others, then the need to quit living by ourselves with those tormenting ghosts of yesterday gets more urgent than ever. We have to talk to somebody about them.

So intense, though, is our fear and reluctance to do this, that many recovering gangster's at first try to bypass Step Five. We search for an easier way which usually consists of the general and fairly painless admission that when committing crimes we were sometimes bad actors. Then, for good measure, we add dramatic descriptions of that part of our criminal behavior which our friends probably know about anyhow. But of the things which really bothered and burned us, we say nothing. Certain distressing or humiliating memories, we tell ourselves, ought not be shared with anyone. These will remain our secret. Not a soul must ever know. We hope they'll go to the grave with us. Yet if recovering gangster's experience means anything at all, this is not only unwise, but it is actually a perilous resolve. Few muddled attitudes have caused us more trouble than holding back on Step Five.

Some people are unable to stay crime free at all; others will relapse periodically until they really clean house. Even recovering gangsters, old-timers, crime free for years, often pay dearly for skipping this Step. They will tell how they tried to carry the load alone; how much they suffered of irritability, anxiety, remorse, and depression; and how, unconsciously seeking relief, they would sometimes accuse even their best friends of the very character defects they themselves were trying to conceal. They always discovered that relief never came by confessing the sins of other people. Everybody had to confess his own. This practice of admitting one's defects to another person is, of course, very ancient. It has been validated in every century, and it characterizes the life of all spiritually centered and truly religious people. But today religion is by no means the sole advocate of this saving principle. Psychiatrists and psychologists point out the deep need every human being has for practical insight and knowledge of his own personality flaws and for a discussion of them with an understanding and trustworthy person. So far as recovering gangsters are concerned, G.A. would go even further. Most of us would declare that without a fearless admission of our defects to another human being we could not stay crime free. It seems plain that the grace of God will not enter to expel our destructive obsessions until we are willing to try this. What are we likely to receive from Step Five? For one thing, we shall get rid of that terrible sense of isolation we've always had. Almost without exception, recovering gangsters are tortured by loneliness. Even before our committing crimes got bad and people began to cut us off, nearly all of us suffered the feeling that we didn't quite belong. Either we were shy, and dared not draw near others, or we were apt to be noisy good fellows craving attention and companionship, but never getting it at least to our way of thinking. There was always that mysterious barrier we could neither get past nor understand. It was as if we were actors on a stage, suddenly realizing that we did not know a single line of our parts. That's one reason we loved criminal behavior so much. It did let us act foolishly. But even that boomeranged on us; we were finally struck down and left in a terrifying loneliness. When we reached the rooms of G.A., and for the first time in our life stood among people who seemed to understand, the sense of belonging was tremendously exciting. We thought the isolation problem had been solved. But we soon discovered that while we weren't alone any more in a social sense, we still suffered from a mental loneliness. Until we talked with complete honesty of our conflicts, and listened to someone else do the same thing, we still didn't belong. Step Five was the answer. It was the beginning of true kinship with man and God. This vital Step was also the means by which we began to get the feeling we could be forgiven, no matter what we once thought or done. Often it was while working on this Step with our sponsors or spiritual advisors that we first felt truly able to forgive others, no matter how deeply we felt they had wronged us.

Our moral inventory persuades us that all around forgiveness is desirable, but it was only when we completely tackled Step Five that we inwardly *knew* we'd be able to receive forgiveness and give it, as well. Another great dividend we may expect from confiding our defects to another human being is humility, a word often misunderstood. To those who have made progress in recovery, it amounts to a clear recognition of what and who we really are, followed by a sincere attempt to become what we could be. Therefore, our first practical move toward humility must consist of recognizing our deficiencies. No defect can be corrected unless we clearly see what it is. But we shall have to do more than *see.* The objective look at ourselves we achieved in Step Four was, after all, only a look. All, for example, recognized a lack of honesty and tolerance we displayed at times with attacks of self pity or delusions of personal superiority. But while this was a humiliating experience, it didn't necessarily mean we had yet acquired much actual humility. Though now recognized, our defects were still there. Something had to be done about them. And we soon found that we could not wish or will them away by ourselves. More realism and therefore more honesty about ourselves are the great gains we make under the influence of Step Five. As we took inventory, we began to suspect how much trouble self delusion had been causing us. This had brought a disturbing reflection. If all our life we had more or less fooled ourselves, how could we now be so sure that we weren't still self deceived? How could we be certain that we had made a true catalog of our defects and had really admitted them, even to ourselves? Because we were still bothered by fear, self pity, and hurt feelings, it was probable we couldn't appraise ourselves fairly at all. Too much guilt and remorse might cause us to dramatize and exaggerate our shortcomings. Our anger and hurt pride might be the smoke screen under which we were hiding some of our defects while we blamed others for them. Possibly, too, we were still handicapped by many liabilities, great and small, we never knew we had.

Hence it was most evident that a solitary self appraisal, and the admission of our defects based upon that alone, wouldn't be nearly enough. We'd have to have outside help if we were surely to know and admit the truth about ourselves we will need the help of God and another human being. Only by discussing ourselves, holding back nothing, being willing to take advice and accept direction could we set foot on the road to straight thinking, solid honesty, and genuine humility. Yet many of us still hung back. We said, "Why can't God as we understand Him tell us where we are astray? If the Creator gave us our life in the first place, then He must know in every detail where we have since gone wrong. Why don't we make our admissions to Him directly? Why do we need to bring anyone else into this?" At this stage, the difficulties of trying to deal rightly with God by ourselves are twofold. Though we may at first be startled to realize that God knows all about us, we are apt to get used to that quite quickly. Somehow, being alone with God doesn't seem as embarrassing as facing up to another person. Until we actually sit down and talk aloud about what we have so long hidden, our willingness to clean house is still just a dream. When we are honest with another person, it confirms that we have been honest with ourselves and with God.

The second difficulty is this: what comes to us alone

may be garbled by our own rationalization and wishful thinking. The benefit of talking to another person is that we can get his direct comment and counsel on our situation, and there can be no doubt in our minds what that advice is. Going it alone in spiritual matters is dangerous. How many times have we heard well intentioned people claim the guidance of God when it was all too plain that they were sorely mistaken? Lacking both practice and humility, they had deluded themselves and were able to justify the most errant nonsense on the ground that this was what God had told them. It is worth noting that people of very high spiritual development almost always insist on sharing with friends or spiritual advisors the guidance they feel they have received from God. Surely, then, a novice ought not lay himself open to the chance of making foolish, perhaps tragic, blunders in this fashion. While the comment or advice of others may by no means be infallible, it is likely to be far more specific than any direct guidance we may receive while we are still so inexperienced in establishing contact with a Power greater than ourselves.

Our next problem will be to discover the person in whom we are to confide. Here we ought to take much care, remembering that prudence is a virtue which carries a high rating. Perhaps we shall need to share facts about ourselves that no others ought to know. We shall want to speak with someone who is experienced, who not only lives crime free but has been able to surmount other serious difficulties. Difficulties, perhaps, like our own. This person may turn out to be one's sponsor, but not necessarily so. If you have developed a high confidence in him, and his temperament and problems are close to your own, then such a choice will be good. Besides, your sponsor already has the advantage of knowing something about your case.

Perhaps, though, your relation to him is such that you would care to reveal only a part of your story. If this is the situation, by all means do so, for you ought to make a beginning as soon as you can. It may turn out, however, that you'll choose someone else for the more difficult and deeper revelations. This individual may be entirely outside of the fellowship. Your clergyman or your doctor, for example. For some of us, a complete stranger may prove the best bet. The real test of the situation is your own willingness to confide and your full confidence in the one with whom you share your first accurate self survey. Even when you've found the person, it frequently takes great resolution to approach him or her. No one ought to say the G.A. program requires no willpower; here is one place where it may require all you've got. Happily, though, the chances are that you will be in for a very pleasant surprise. When your mission is carefully explained, and it is seen by the recipient of your confidence, how helpful he can really be, the conversation will start easily and will soon become eager. Before long, your listener may well tell a story or two about himself which will place you even more at ease. Provided you hold back nothing, your sense of relief will mount from minute to minute. The dammed up emotions hold in for years break out of their confinement, and miraculously vanish as soon as they are exposed. As the pain subsides, a healing tranquility takes its place. And when humility and serenity are so combined, something else of greatness is apt to occur. Many a recovering gangster, once agnostic or atheistic, tells us that it was during this stage of Step Five that he first actually felt the presence of God. And even those who had faith already often become more conscious of God as they never were before. This feeling of being at one with God and man, this emerging from isolation through the open and honest sharing of our terrible burden of guilt, brings us to a resting place where we may prepare ourselves for the following Steps toward a full and meaningful crime free living.

STEP SIX

"We were entirely ready to have God remove all these defects of character."

Why ask for something before we are ready for it? This would be asking for trouble. So many times gangsters have sought the rewards of hard work without the labor. Willingness is what we strive for in Step Six. How sincerely we work this step will be proportionate to our desire for change. Do we really want to be free of our resentments, our anger, and our fear? Many of us cling to our fears, doubts, self-loathing or hatred because there is a certain distorted security in familiar pain. It seems safer to embrace what we know than to let go of it for the unknown.

Letting go of character defects must be decisive. We suffer because their demands weaken us. If we were proud, we now find that we cannot get away with arrogance. If we are not humble, we are humiliated. If we are greedy, we find that we are never satisfied. Before taking Steps Four and Five, we could indulge in fear, anger, dishonesty or self-pity. Now indulgence in these character defects clouds our ability to think logically. Selfishness becomes an intolerable, destructive chain that ties us to our bad habits.

Our defects drain us of all our time and energy.

We examine the Fourth Step inventory and got a good look at what these defects are doing to our life. We begin to long for freedom from these defects. We pray or otherwise become willing, ready and able to let God remove these destructive traits. We need a personality change, if we are to stay crime free. We want to change. We should approach old defects with an open mind. We are aware of them and yet we still make the same mistakes and are unable to break the bad habits. We look to the Fellowship for the kind of life that we want for ourselves. We ask our friends, "Did you let go?" Almost without exception the answer is, "Yes, to the best of my ability."

When we see how our defects exist in our life and accept them, we can let go of them and get on with our new life. We learn that we are growing when we make new mistakes instead of repeating old ones. When we are working Step Six, it is important to remember that we are human and should not place unrealistic expectations on ourselves. This is a step of willingness. Willingness is the spiritual principle of Step Six. Step Six helps us move in a spiritual direction. Being human, we will wander off course.

Rebellion is a character defect that ruins us here. We need not lose faith when we become rebellious. Rebellion can produce indifference or intolerance, which can be triumphed over by persistent effort. We keep asking for willingness. We may be doubtful that God will see fit to relieve us or that something will go wrong. We ask another member who says, "You're right where you're supposed to be. We renew our readiness to have our defects removed. We surrender to the simple suggestions that the program offers us. Even though we are not entirely ready, we are in the right direction.

Eventually faith, humility and acceptance replace pride and rebellion. We come to know ourselves. We find ourselves growing into mature consciousness. We begin to feel better, as willingness grows into hope. Perhaps for the first time, we see a vision of our new life. With this in sight, we put our willingness into action by moving on to Step Seven.

Step Six is the Step that separates the men from the boys." So declares a well loved clergyman who happens to be one of the recovering gangsters' greatest friends. He goes on to explain that any person capable of enough willingness and honesty to repeatedly try Step Six on all his faults *without any reservations whatever* has indeed come a long way spiritually, and is therefore entitled to be called a man who is sincerely trying to grow in the image and likeness of his own Creator.

Of course, the often disputed question of whether God can and will, under certain conditions, remove defects of character will be answered with a prompt affirmative by almost any recovering gangster. To him, this proposition will be no theory at all; it will be just about the largest fact in his life. He will usually offer his proof in a statement like this:

"Sure, I was beaten, absolutely licked. My own willpower just wouldn't work on criminal behavior. Change of scene, the best efforts of family, friends, doctors, and clergymen got no place with my criminal behaviorism. I simply couldn't stop committing crimes, and no human being could seem to do the job for me. But when I became willing to clean house and then asked a Higher Power, God as I understood Him, to give me release, my obsession to commit crimes vanished. It was lifted right out of me." In G.A. meetings all over the world, statements just like these are heard daily. It is plain for everybody to see that each crime free recovering gangster has been granted a release from this very obstinate and potentially fatal obsession. So in a very complete and literal way, all recovering gangsters' have "become entirely ready" to have God remove the mania for criminal behavior from their life. And God has proceeded to do exactly that.

Having been granted a perfect release from criminal behaviorism, why then shouldn't we be able to achieve by the same means a perfect release from every other difficulty or defect? This is a riddle of our existence, the full answer to which may be only in the mind of God. Nevertheless, at least a part of the answer to it is apparent to us. When men and women pour so much criminal behavior into themselves that they destroy their life, they commit a most unnatural act. Defying their instinctive desire for self preservation, they seem bent upon self destruction. They work against their own deepest instinct. As they are humbled by the terrific beating administered by criminal behavior, the grace of God can enter them and expel their obsession. Here their powerful instinct to live can cooperate fully with their Creator's desire to give them new life. For nature and God alike abhor suicide. But most of our other difficulties don't fall under such a category at all. Every normal person wants, for example, to eat, to reproduce, to be somebody in the society of his fellows. And he wishes to be reasonably safe and secure as he tries to attain these things. Indeed, God made him that way. He did not design man to destroy himself with criminal behavior, but He did give man instincts to help him to stay alive. It is nowhere evident, at least in this life, that our Creator expects us fully to eliminate our instinctual drives. So far as we know, it is nowhere on the record that God has completely removed from any human being all his natural drives.

Since most of us are born with an abundance of natural desires, it isn't strange that we often let these far exceed their intended purpose. When they drive us blindly, or we willfully demand that they supply us with more satisfactions or pleasures than are possible or due us, that is the point at which we depart from the degree of perfection that God wishes for us here on earth. That is the measure of our character defects, or, if you wish, of our sins. If we ask, God will certainly forgive our dereliction. But in no case does He render us white as snow and keep us that way without our cooperation. That is something we are supposed to be willing to work toward ourselves. He asks only that we try as best we know how to make progress in the building of our new character.

So Step Six "We're entirely ready to have God remove all these defects of character" is a recovering gangsters' way of stating that this is the best possible attitude one can take in order to make a beginning on this lifetime job. This does not mean that we expect all our character defects to be lifted out of us as the drive to commit crimes was. A few of them may be, but with most of them we shall have to be content with patient improvement. The key words "entirely ready" underline the fact that we want to aim at the very best we know or can learn. How many of us have this degree of readiness? In an absolute sense practically nobody has it. The best we can do, with all the honesty that we can summon, is to *try* to have it. Even then the best of us will discover to our dismay that there is always a sticking point, a point at which we say, "No, I can't give this up yet." And we shall often tread on even more dangerous ground when we cry, "This I will *never* give up!" Such is the power of our instincts to over reach it. No matter how far we have progressed, desires will always be found that oppose the grace of God.

Some who feel they have done well may dispute this, so let's try to think it through a little further. Practically everybody wishes to be rid of his most glaring and destructive handicaps. No one wants to be so proud that he is scorned as a braggart, nor so greedy that he is labeled a thief. No one wants to be angry enough to murder, lustful enough to rape, gluttonous enough to ruin his health. No one wants to be agonized by the chronic pain of envy or to be paralyzed by sloth. Of course, most human beings don't suffer these defects at these rock bottom levels.

We who have escaped these extremes are apt to congratulate ourselves. Yet can we? After all, hasn't it been self interest, pure and simple, that has enabled most of us to escape? Not much spiritual effort is involved in avoiding excesses which will bring us punishment anyway. But when we face up to the less violent aspects of these very same defects, *then* where do we stand? What we must recognize now is that we live in some of our defects. We really love them. Who, for example, doesn't like to feel just a little superior to the next fellow, or even quite a lot superior? Isn't it true that we like to let greed masquerade as ambition? To think of *liking* lust seems impossible. But how many men and women speak love with their lips, and believe what they say, in order to hide lust in a dark corner of their minds? And even while staying within conventional bounds, many people have to admit that their imaginary sexual excursions are apt to be all dressed up as dreams of romance. Self-righteous anger also can be very enjoyable. In a perverse way we can actually take satisfaction from the fact that many people annoy us, for it brings a comfortable feeling of superiority. Gossip barbed with our anger, a polite form of murder by character assassination, has its satisfactions for us, too. Here we are not trying to help those we criticize; we are trying to proclaim our own righteousness.

When greediness is less than harmful, we have a milder word for that, too; we call it "coming up." We live in a world riddled with criminal minded people. To a greater or less degree, everybody is infected with it. From this defect we must surely get a warped yet definite satisfaction. Or else why would we consume such great amounts of time wishing for what we have not, rather than working for it, or angrily looking for attributes we shall never have, instead of adjusting to the fact, and accepting it? How often we work hard with no better motive than to be secured and become slothful later on. We call that "retiring." Consider, too, our talents for procrastination, which is really sloth in five syllables. Nearly anyone could submit a good list of such defects as these, and few of us would seriously think of giving them up. We might become miserable.

Some people, of course, may conclude that they are indeed ready to have all such defects taken from them. But even these people, if they construct a list of still milder defects, will be obliged to admit that they prefer to hang on to *some* of them. Therefore, it seems plain that few of us can quickly or easily become ready to aim at spiritual and moral perfection; we want to settle for only as much perfection as will get us by in life, according, of course, to our various and sundry ideas of what will get us by. So the difference between "the boys and the men" is the difference between striving for a self determined objective and for the perfect objective which is of God.

Many will at once ask, "How *can* we accept the entire implication of Step Six? Why that is *perfection!*" This sounds like a hard question, but practically speaking, it isn't. Only Step One, where we made the one hundred percent admission we were powerless over criminal behavior, can be practiced with absolute perfection. The remaining eleven Steps state perfect ideals. They are goals toward which we look, and the measuring sticks by which we estimate our progress. Seen in this light, Step Six is still difficult, but not at all impossible. The only urgent thing is that we make a beginning, and keep trying.

If we would gain any real advantage in this Step on problems other than criminal behavior, we shall need to make a brand new venture into open mindedness. We shall need to raise our eyes toward perfection, and be ready to walk in that direction. It will seldom matter how haltingly we walk. The only question will be, "are we ready?" Looking again at those defects we are still unwilling to give up, we ought to erase the hard and fast lines that we have drawn. Perhaps we shall be obliged in some cases still **to** say, "This I cannot give up yet," but we should not say to ourselves, "This I will *never* give up!"

Let's dispose of what appears to be a hazardous open end we have left. It is suggested that we ought to become entirely willing to aim toward perfection. We note that some delay, however, might be pardoned. That word, in the mind of a rationalizing recovering gangster, could certainly be given a long term meaning. He could say, "How very easy! Sure, I'll head toward perfection, but I'm certainly not going to hurry any. Maybe I can postpone dealing with some of my problems indefinitely." Of course, this won't do. Such a bluffing of oneself will have to go the way of many another pleasant rationalization. At the very least, we shall have to come to grips with some of our worst character defects and take action toward their removal as quickly as we can. The moment we say, "No, never!", our minds close against the grace of God. Delay is dangerous, and rebellion may be fatal. This is the exact point at which we abandon our limited objectives, and move toward God's will for us.

STEP SEVEN

"We humbly asked Him to remove our shortcomings."

Character defects or shortcomings are those things that cause pain and misery all of our life. If they contributed to our health and happiness, we would not have come to such a state of desperation. We had to become ready to have God, as we understood Him, remove these defects. Having decided that we want God to relieve us of the useless or destructive aspects of our personalities, we have arrived at the Seventh Step. We could not handle the ordeal of life all by ourselves. It was not until we made a real mess of our life that we realized we could not do it alone. By admitting this, we achieved a glimpse of humility. This is the main ingredient of Step Seven. Humility is a result of getting honest with ourselves. We have practiced being honest since Step One. We accepted our gangster's mentality and powerlessness. We found strength beyond ourselves and learned to rely on it. We examined our life and discovered who we really are. To be truly humble is to accept and honestly try to be ourselves. None of us is perfectly good or perfectly bad. We are people who have assets and liabilities. Most importantly, we are human. Humility is as much a part of staying crime free as food and water are to staying alive. As our gangster mentality progressed, we devoted our energy toward satisfying our material desires. All other needs were beyond our reach. We always wanted gratification of our basic desires. The Seventh Step is an action step, and it is time to ask God for help and relief.   We have to understand that our way of thinking is not the only way; other people can give us direction. When someone points out a shortcoming, our first reaction may be defensive. We must realize that we are not perfect. There will always be room for growth. If we truly want to be free, we will take a good look at input from fellow recovering gangsters. If the shortcomings we discover are real, and we have a chance to exonerate them, we will surely experience a sense of well-being.

Some will want to get on their knees for this step.

Some will be very quiet, and others will put forth a great emotional effort to show intense willingness. The word humble applies because we approach this Power greater than ourselves to ask for the freedom to live without the limitations of our past ways. Many of us are willing to work this step without reservations, on pure blind faith, because we are sick of what we have been doing and how we are feeling. Whatever works, we go all the way. This is our road to spiritual growth. We change every day. We gradually and carefully pull ourselves out of the isolation and loneliness of our gangster mentality and into the mainstream of life. This growth is not the result of wishing, but of action and prayer. The main objective of Step 7 is to get out of ourselves and strive to achieve the will of our Higher Power. If we are careless and fail to grasp the spiritual meaning of this step, we may have difficulties and stir up old troubles. One danger is in being too hard on ourselves. Sharing with other recovering gangsters will help us to avoid becoming morbidly serious about ourselves. Accepting the defects of others can help us become humble and pave the way for our own defects to be relieved.

God often works through those who care enough about recovery to help make us aware of our shortcomings. We have noticed that humility plays a big part in this program and our new way of life. We take our inventory; we become ready to let God remove our defects of character; we humbly ask Him to remove our shortcomings. This is our road to spiritual growth, and we will want to continue.

We are ready for Step Eight. Since this Step so specifically concerns itself with humility, we should pause here to consider what humility is and what the practice of it can mean to us.

Indeed, the attainment of greater humility is the foundational principle of each of G.A. Twelve Step. For without some degree of humility, no recovering gangster can stay crime free at all. Nearly all members have found, too, that unless they develop much more of this precious quality which is required just for crime free living, they still haven't much chance of becoming truly happy. Without it, they cannot live to much useful purpose, or, in adversity, be able to summon the faith that can meet any emergency.

Humility, as a word and as an ideal, has a very bad time of it in our world. Not only is the idea misunderstood; the word itself is often intensely disliked. Many people haven't even a nodding acquaintance with humility as a way of life. Much of the everyday talk we hear, and a great deal of what we read, high lit man's pride in his own achievements. With great intelligence, men of science have been forcing nature to disclose her secrets. The immense resources now being harnessed promise such a quantity of material blessings that many have come to believe that a man made millennium lies just ahead. Poverty will disappear, and there will be such abundance that everybody can have all the security and personal satisfactions he desires. The theory seems to be that once everybody's primary instincts are satisfied, there won't be much left to quarrel about. The world will then turn happy and be free to concentrate on culture and character. Solely by their own intelligence and labor, men will have shaped their own destiny.

Certainly no recovering gangster, and surely no member of G.A., wants to deprecate material achievement. Nor do we enter into debate with the many that still so passionately cling to the belief that to satisfy our basic natural desires is the main object of life. But we are sure that no class of people in the world ever made a worse mess of trying to live by this formula than recovering gangsters. For thousands of years man has been demanding more than our share of security, prestige, and romance. When we seemed to be succeeding, we then committed crimes to dream still greater dreams. When we were frustrated, even in part, we committed crimes for oblivion. Never was there enough of what we thought we wanted.

In all these strivings, so many of them well intentioned, our crippling handicap had been our lack of humility. We had lacked the perspective to see that character building and spiritual values had to come first, and that material satisfactions were not the purpose of living. Quite characteristically, we had gone all out in confusing the ends with the means. Instead of regarding the satisfaction of our material desires as the means by which we could live and function as human beings, we had taken these satisfactions to be the final end and aim of life.

True, most of us thought good character was

desirable, but obviously good character was something one needed to get on with the business of being self satisfied. With a proper display of honesty and morality, we'd stand a better chance of getting what we really wanted. But whenever we had to choose between character and comfort, the character building was lost in the dust of our chase after what we thought was happiness. Seldom did we look at character building as something desirable in itself, something we would like to strive for whether our instinctual needs were met or not. We never thought of making honesty, tolerance, and true love of man and God the daily basis of living.

This lack of anchorage to any permanent values, this blindness to the true purpose of our life, produced another bad result. For just so long as we were convinced that we could live exclusively by our own individual strength and intelligence, for just that long was a working faith in a Higher Power impossible. This was true even when we believed that God existed. We could actually have earnest religious beliefs which remained barren because we were still trying to play God ourselves. As long as we placed self-reliance first, a genuine reliance upon a Higher Power was out of the question. That basic ingredient of all humility, a desire to seek and do God's will, was missing.

For us, the process of gaining a new perspective was unbelievably painful. It was only by repeated humiliations that we were forced to learn something about humility. It was only at the end of a long road, marked by successive defeats and humiliations, and the final crushing of our self-sufficiency that we began to feel humility as something more than a condition of groveling despair. Every newcomer in recovery is told, and soon realizes for himself, that his humble admission of powerlessness over criminal is his first step toward liberation from its paralyzing grip.

So it is that we first see humility as a necessity. But this is the barest beginning. To get completely away from our aversion to the idea of being humble, to gain a vision of humility as the avenue to true freedom of the human spirit, to be willing to work for humility as something to be desired for itself, takes most of us a long, long time. A whole lifetime geared to self-centeredness cannot be set in reverse all at once. Rebellion dogs our every step at first.

When we have finally admitted without reservation that we are powerless over criminal, we are apt to breathe a great sigh of relief, saying, "Well, thank God that's over! I'll never have to go through that again!" Then we learn, often to our consternation, that this is only the first milestone on the new road we are walking. Still goaded by sheer necessity, we reluctantly come to grips with those serious character flaws that made problem drinkers of us in the first place, flaws which must be dealt with to prevent a retreat into criminal behavior once again. We will want to be rid of some of these defects, but in some instances this will appear to be an impossible job from which we recoil. And we cling with a passionate persistence to others which are just as disturbing to our equilibrium, because we still enjoy them too much. How can we possibly summon the resolution and the willingness to get rid of such overwhelming compulsions and desires? But again we are driven on by the inescapable conclusion which we draw from the memberships experience, that we surely must try with a will, or else fall by the wayside. At this stage of our progress we are under heavy pressure and coercion to do the right thing. We are obliged to choose between the pains of trying and the certain penalties of failing to do so. These initial steps along the road are taken grudgingly, yet we do take them. We may still have no very high opinion of humility as a desirable personal virtue, but we do recognize it as a necessary aid to our survival.

But when we have taken a square look at some of these defects, have discussed them with another, and have become willing to have them removed, our thinking about humility commences to have a wider meaning. By this time in all probability we have gained some measure of release from our more devastating handicaps. We enjoy moments in which there is something like real peace of mind. To those of us who have hitherto known only excitement, depression, or anxiety in other words, to this newfound peace is a priceless gift. Something new indeed has been added. Where humility had formerly stood for a forced feeding off humble pie, it now creates a new meaning, the nourishing ingredient which can give us serenity.

This improved perception of humility starts another revolutionary change in our outlook. Our eyes begin to open to the immense values which have come straight out of painful ego puncturing. Until now, our life have been largely devoted to running from pain and problems. We fled from them as from a plague. We never wanted to deal with the fact of suffering. Escape via the bottle was always our solution. Character building through suffering might be all right for saints, but it certainly didn't appeal to us. Then, in G.A., we looked and listened. Everywhere we saw failure and misery transformed by humility into priceless assets. We heard story after story of how humility had brought strength out of weakness. In every case, pain had been the price of admission into a new life. But this admission price had purchased more than we expected. It brought a measure of humility, which we soon discovered to be a healer of pain. We began to fear pain less, and desire humility more than ever.

During this process of learning more about humility, the most profound result of all was the change in our attitude toward God. And this was true whether we had been believers or unbelievers. We began to get over the idea that the Higher Power was a sort of major-league pinch hitter, to be called upon only in an emergency. The notion that we would still live our own life, God helping a little now and then, began to evaporate. Many of us who had thought ourselves religious awoke to the limitations of this attitude. Refusing to place God first, we had deprived ourselves of His help. But now the words "Of myself I am nothing, the Father doeth the works" began to carry bright promise and meaning.

We saw we needn't always be bludgeoned and beaten into humility. It could come quite as much from our voluntary reaching for it as it could from unremitting suffering. A great turning point in our life came when we sought for humility as something we really wanted, rather than as something we must have. It marked the time when we could commence to see the full implication of Step Seven: "Humbly asked Him to remove our shortcomings."

As we approach the actual taking of Step Seven, it might be well if we inquire once more just what our deeper objectives are. Each of us would like to live at peace with himself and with his fellow man. We would like to be assured that the grace of God can do for us what we cannot do for ourselves. We have seen that character defects based upon shortsighted or unworthy desires are the obstacles that block our path toward these objectives. We now clearly see that we have been making unreasonable demands upon ourselves, upon others, and upon God.

The chief activator of our defects has been self-centered fear primarily, fear that we would lose something we already possessed or would fail to get something we demanded. Living upon a basis of unsatisfied demands, we were in a state of continual disturbance and frustration. Therefore, no peace was to be had unless we could find a means of reducing these demands. The difference between a demand and a simple request is plain to anyone.

The Seventh Step is where we make the change in our attitude that permits us, with humility as our guide, to move out from ourselves toward others and toward God. The whole emphasis of Step Seven is on humility. It is really saying to us that we now ought to be willing to try humility in seeking the removal of our other shortcomings just as we did when we admitted that we were powerless over criminal, and came to believe that a Power greater than ourselves could restore us to sanity. If that degree of humility could enable us to find the grace by which such a deadly obsession could be banished, then there must be hope of the same result respecting any other problem we could possibly have.

STEP EIGHT

"We made a list of all persons we had harmed, and became willing to make amends to them all."

Step Eight is the test of our newfound humility. Our purpose is to achieve freedom from the guilt we have carried. We want to look the world in the eye with neither aggressiveness nor fear. Are we willing to make a list of all persons we had harmed to clear away the fear and guilt that our past holds for us? Our experience tells us that we must become willing to do this before this step will have any effect. The Eighth Step is not easy; it demands a new kind of honesty about our relations with other people. The Eighth Step starts the process of forgiveness. We forgive others; and finally we forgive ourselves and learn how to live in the world. By the time we reach this step, we have become ready to understand. We can live and let live easier when we know the areas in which we owe amends. It seems hard now, but once we do it, we will wonder why we did not do it long ago.

We need real honesty before we can make an accurate list. In preparing to make the list, it is helpful to define harm. One definition of harm is physical or mental damage. Another definition of harm is inflicting pain, suffering or loss, the damage done by something that is said, done or left undone. Harm can result from words or actions, either intentional or unintentional. The degree of harm can range from making someone feel mentally uncomfortable to inflicting bodily injury or even death. The Eighth Step presents us with a problem. Many of us have difficulty admitting that we caused harm for others, because we thought we were victims of our gangsters' mentality. Avoiding this rationalization is crucial to the Eighth Step. We must separate what was done to us from what we did to others. We cut away our justifications and our ideas of being a victim. We often feel that we only harmed enemies, yet we usually list ourselves last, if at all.

This step is doing the legwork to repair the wreckage of our old behavior. It will not make us better people to judge the faults of another. It will make us feel better to clean up our history by relieving ourselves of guilt. By writing our list, we can no longer deny that we caused harm. We admit that we hurt others, directly or indirectly, through some action, lie, broken promise or neglect. We make our list, or take it from our Fourth Step, and add additional people as we think of them. We face this list honestly, and openly examine our faults so we can become willing to make amends. In some cases, we may not know the persons that we have wronged. While under the influence of our gangster mentality anyone that we came in contact was at risk. Many members mention their parents, spouses, children, friends, lovers, other gangsters, casual acquaintances, co-workers, employers, teachers, property owners and total strangers. We may also place ourselves on the list, because while practicing our gangsters' mentality, we were slowly killing ourselves.

We may find it beneficial to make a separate list of people to whom we owe financial amends. As with each step, we must be thorough, most of us fall short of our goals more often than we exceed them. At the same time, we cannot put off the completion of this step just because we are not sure that our list is complete. We are never finished. The final difficulty in working the Eighth Step is separating it from the Ninth Step. Projections about actually making amends can be a major obstacle both in making the list and in becoming willing. We do this step as if there were no Ninth Step. We do not even think about making the amends but just concentrate on exactly what the Eighth Step says, make a list and become willing. The main device this step has for us is to help build awareness that, little by little, we are gaining new attitudes about ourselves and how we deal with other people. Listening carefully to other member's share their experience regarding this step can relieve any confusion that we may have about writing our list. In addition, our sponsors may share with us how Step Eight worked for them. Asking a question during a meeting can give us the benefit of group conscience.

The Eighth Step offers a big change from a life dominated by guilt and remorse. Our futures are changed, because we do not have to avoid those who we have harmed. Because of this step, we receive a new freedom that can end isolation. As we realize our need to be forgiven, we tend to be more forgiving. At least, we know that we are no longer intentionally making life miserable for people. The Eighth Step is an action step. Like all the steps, it offers immediate benefits. We are now free to begin our amends in Step Nine. Steps Eight and Nine are concerned with personal relations. First, we take a look backward and try to discover where we have been at fault; next we make a vigorous attempt to repair the damage we have done; and third, having thus cleaned away the debris of the past, we consider how, with our newfound knowledge of ourselves, we may develop the best possible relations with every human being we know.

This is a very large order. It is a task which we may perform with increasing skill, but never really finish. Learning how to live in the greatest peace, partnership, and brotherhood with all men and women, of whatever description, is a moving and fascinating adventure. Every recovering gangster has found that he can make little headway in this new adventure of living until he first backtracks and really makes an accurate and unsparing survey of the human wreckage he has left in his wake. To a degree, he has already done this when taking moral inventory, but now the time has come when he ought to redouble his efforts to see how many people he has hurt, and in what ways. This reopening of emotional wounds, some old, some perhaps forgotten, and some still painfully festering, will at first look like a purposeless and pointless piece of surgery. But if a willing start is made, then the great advantages of doing this will quickly reveal themselves that the pain will be lessened as one obstacle after another melts away.

These obstacles, however, are very real. The first, and one of the most difficult, has to do with forgiveness. The moment we ponder a brutal beating against another person, our emotions go on the defensive. To escape looking at the wrongs we have done another, we resentfully focus on the wrong that was done us. This is especially true if the newcomer has, in fact, behaved very badly at all. Triumphantly we seize upon others misbehavior as the perfect excuse for minimizing or forgetting our own.

Here we need to fetch ourselves up sharply. It doesn't make much sense when a real tosspot calls a kettle black. Let's remember that recovering gangsters are not the only ones bedeviled by sick emotions. Moreover, it is usually a fact that our behavior when committing crimes in our communities has aggravated the defects of others. We've repeatedly strained the patience of our community to a snapping point, and have brought out the very worst in those who didn't think much of us to begin with. In many instances we are really dealing with fellow sufferers, people whose woes we have increased. If we are now about to ask forgiveness for ourselves, why shouldn't we start out by forgiving them, one and all? When listing the people we have harmed, most of us hit another solid obstacle. We got a pretty severe shock when we realized that we were preparing to make a face to face admission of our wretched conduct to those we had hurt. It had been embarrassing enough when, in confidence, we had admitted these things to God, to ourselves, and to another human being. But the prospect of actually visiting or even writing the people concerned now overwhelm us, especially when we remembered in what poor favor we stood with most of them. There were cases, too, where we had damaged others who were still happily unaware of being hurt. Why, we cried, shouldn't bygones be bygones? Why do we have to think of these people at all? These were some of the ways in which fear conspired with pride to hinder our making a list of all the people we had harmed.

Some of us, though, tripped over a very different snag. We clung to the claim that when committing crimes we never hurt anybody but ourselves. Our families didn't suffer, because we always paid the bills and seldom committed crimes at home. Our crime partners didn't suffer, because we were usually on the job. Our reputations hadn't suffered, because we were certain few knew of our crimes. Those who did would sometimes assure us that, after all, poverty was not their fault therefore crime was only a good man's fault. What real harm, therefore, had we done? No more, surely, than we could easily mend with a few casual apologies, or our lifetime in prison.

This attitude, of course, is the end result of purposeful forgetting. It is an attitude which can only be changed by a deep and honest search of our motives and actions.

In some cases we cannot make restitution at all, and in some cases action ought to be deferred; however we should nevertheless make an accurate and really exhaustive survey of our past life as it has affected other people. In many instances we shall find that though the harm done others was infinitely great, the emotional harm we have done ourselves has been even more so extraordinary. Very deep, sometimes quite forgotten, damaging emotional conflicts persist below the level of consciousness. At the time of these occurrences, they may actually have given our emotions violent twists which have since discolored our personalities and altered our life for the worse.

While the purpose of making restitution to others is paramount, it is equally necessary that we extricate from an examination of our personal relations every bit of information about ourselves and our fundamental difficulties that we can. Since defective relations with other human beings have nearly always been the immediate cause of our woes, including our crimes, no field of investigation could yield more satisfying and valuable rewards than this one. Calm, thoughtful reflection upon personal relations can deepen our insight. We can go far beyond those things which were superficially wrong with us, to see those flaws which were basic, flaws sometimes were responsible for the whole pattern of our life. Thoroughness, we have found, will pay and pay handsomely.

We might next ask ourselves what we mean when we say that we have "harmed" other people. What kinds of "harm" do to people do one another, anyway? To define the word "harm" in a practical way, we might call it the result of instincts in collision, which cause physical, mental, emotional, or spiritual damage to people. If our tempers are consistently bad, we arouse anger in others. If we lie or cheat, we deprive others not only of their worldly goods, but of their emotional security and peace of mind. We really issue them an invitation to become contemptuous and vengeful. If our sexual conduct is selfish, we may excite jealousy, misery, and a strong desire to retaliate in kind.

Such gross misbehavior is not by any means a full catalogue of the harms we do. Let us think of some of the subtler ones that can sometimes be quite as damaging. Suppose that in our family life we happen to be miserable, irresponsible, callous, or cold. Suppose that we are irritable, critical, impatient, and humorless. Suppose we lavish attention upon one member of the family and neglect the others. What happens when we try to dominate the whole family, either by a rule of iron fist or by a constant outpouring of minute directions for just how their life should be lived from hour to hour? What happens when we wallow in depression, self pity oozing from every pore, and inflict that upon those around us? Such a roster of harms done others the kind that make daily living with us as practicing recovering gangsters difficult and often unbearable could be extended almost indefinitely. When we take such personality traits as these into the class, the work place, and the society of our fellows, they can do damage almost as extensive as what we have caused at home.

Having carefully surveyed this whole area of human relations, and having decided exactly what personality traits in us injured and disturbed others, we can now commence to ransack our memory for the people to whom we have given offense. To put a finger on the nearby and most deeply damaged ones shouldn't be hard to do. Then, as year by year we walk back through our life as far as our memory will reach, we shall be bound to construct a long list of people who have, to some extent or other, been affected. We should, of course, ponder and weigh each instance carefully. We shall want to hold ourselves to the course of admitting the things we have done, meanwhile forgiving the wrongs done us, real or imagined. We should avoid extreme judgments, both of ourselves and of anyone involved. We must not exaggerate our defects or theirs. A quiet, objective view will be our steadfast aim.

Whenever our pencil falters, we can fortify and cheer

ourselves on by remembering what the G. A. experience in this Step has meant to others. It is the beginning of the end of isolation from our fellows and from God.

STEP NINE

"We made direct amends to such people wherever possible, except when to do so would injure them or others."

This step should not be avoided. If we do, we are reserving a place in our program for a relapse. Pride, fear and procrastination often seem an impossible barrier; they stand in the way of progress and growth. The important thing is to take action and to be ready to accept the reactions of those persons we have harmed. We make amends to the best of our ability. Timing is an essential part of this step. We should make amends when the opportunity presents itself, except when to do so will cause more harm. Sometimes we cannot actually make the amends; it is neither possible nor practical. In some cases, amends may be beyond our means. We find that willingness can serve in the place of action where we are unable to contact the person that we have harmed. However, we should never fail to contact anyone because of embarrassment, fear or procrastination. We want to be free of our guilt, but we do not wish to do so at the expense of anyone else. We might run the risk of involving a third person or some companion from our criminal days who does not wish to be exposed. We do not have the right or the need to endanger another person. It is often necessary to take guidance from others in these matters.

We recommend turning our legal problems over to lawyers and our financial or medical problems to professionals. Part of learning how to live successfully is learning when we need help. In some old relationships, an unresolved conflict may still exist. We do our part to resolve old conflicts by making our amends. We want to step away from further antagonisms and ongoing resentments. In many instances, we can only go to the person and humbly ask for understanding of past wrongs. Sometimes this will be a joyous occasion when old friends or relatives prove willing to let go of their bitterness. Contacting someone who is still hurting from the burn of our misdeeds can be dangerous. Indirect amends may be necessary where direct ones would be unsafe or endanger other people. We make our amends to the best of our ability. We try to remember that when we make amends, we are doing it for ourselves. Instead of feeling guilty and remorseful, we feel relieved about our past. We accept that it was our actions that caused our negative attitude. Step Nine helps us with our guilt and helps others with their anger. Sometimes, the only amends we can make is to stay crime-free. We owe it to ourselves and to our loved ones.

We are no longer making a mess in society because of our need to commit crimes.

Sometimes the only way we can make amends is to contribute to society. Now, we are helping ourselves and other gangsters to recover. This is a tremendous amendment to the whole community. In the process of our recovery, we are restored to sanity and part of our sanity is effectively relating to others. We less often view people as a threat to our security. Real security will replace the physical ache and mental confusion that we have experienced in the past. We approach those we have harmed with humility and patience. Many of our sincere well-wishers may be reluctant to accept our recovery as real. We must remember the pain that they have known. In time, many miracles will occur. Many of us who were separated from our families succeed in establishing relationships with them. Eventually it becomes easier for them to accept the change in us. Crime free time speaks for itself. Patience is an important part of our recovery. The unconditional love we experience will rejuvenate our will to live, and each positive move on our part will be matched by an unexpected opportunity. A lot of courage and faith goes into making amends, and spiritual growth is the result. We are achieving freedom from the wreckage of our past. We will want to keep our house in order by practicing a continuous personal inventory in Step Ten. Good judgment, a careful sense of timing, courage, and prudence, these are the qualities we shall need when we take Step Nine.

After we have made the list of people we have harmed, have reflected carefully upon each instance, and have tried to possess ourselves of the right attitude in which to proceed, we will see that the making of direct amends divides those we should approach into several classes. There will be those who ought to be dealt with just as soon as we become reasonably confident that we can maintain our crime free living. There will be those to whom we can make only partial restitution, lest complete disclosures do them or others more harm than good. There will be other cases where action ought to be deferred, and still others in which by the very nature of the situation we shall never be able to make direct personal contact at all.

Most of us begin making certain kinds of direct amends from the day we join Gangsters Anonymous. The moment we tell our families that we are really going to try the program, the process has begun. In this area there are seldom any questions of timing or caution. We want to come in the door shouting the good news. After coming from our first meeting, or perhaps after we have finished reading the book, "Gangsters Anonymous," we usually want to sit down with some member of the family and readily admit the damage we have done as a result of our criminal behavior. Almost always we want to go further and admit other defects that have made us hard to live with. This will be a very different occasion, and in sharp contrast with those hangover mornings when we alternated between reviling ourselves and blaming the family (and everyone else) for our troubles. At this first sitting, it is necessary only that we make a general admission of our defects. It may be unwise at this stage to rehash certain harrowing episodes. Good judgment will suggest that we ought to take our time. While we may be quite willing to reveal the very worst, we must be sure to remember that we cannot buy our own peace of mind at the expense of others. The same approach will apply at the office or factory. We shall at once think of a few people who know all about our criminal acts, and who have been most affected by it. But even in these cases, we may need to use a little more discretion than we did with the family. We may not want to say anything for several weeks, or longer. First, we will wish to be reasonably certain that we are on the G.A. beam. Then we are ready to go to these people, explain what G.A. is, and what we are trying to do. Against this background we can freely admit the damage we have done and make our apologies. We can pay, or promise to pay, whatever obligations, financial or otherwise, we owe. The generous response of most people to such quiet sincerity will often astonish us. Even our severest and most justified critics will frequently meet us more than halfway on the first trial.

This atmosphere of approval and praise is apt to be so exhilarating as to put us off balance by creating an insatiable appetite for more of the same. Or we may be tipped over in the other direction when, in rare cases, we get a cool and skeptical reception. This will tempt us to argue, or to press our point insistently. Or maybe it will tempt us toward discouragement and pessimism. But if we have prepared ourselves well in advance such reactions will not deflect us from our steady and even purpose.

After taking this preliminary trial at making amends, we may enjoy such a sense of relief that we may think our task is finished. We will want to rest on our laurels. The temptation to skip the more humiliating and dreaded meetings that still remain may be great. We will often manufacture plausible excuses for dodging these issues entirely. Or we may just procrastinate; telling ourselves the time is not yet, when in reality we have already passed up many a fine chance to right a serious wrong. Let's not talk prudence while practicing evasion.

As soon as we begin to feel confident in our new way of life and have begun, by our behavior and example, to convince those about us that we are indeed changing for the better, it is usually safe to talk in complete frankness with those who have been seriously affected, even those who may be only a little or not at all aware of what we have done to them. The only exceptions we will make will be cases where our disclosure would cause actual harm. These conversations can begin in a casual or natural way. But if no such opportunity presents itself, at some point we will want to summon all our courage, head straight for the person concerned, and lay our cards on the table. We needn't wallow in excessive remorse before those we have harmed, but amends at this level should always be forthright and generous.

There can only be one consideration which should qualify our desire for a complete disclosure of the damage we have done. That will arise in the occasional situation where to make a full revelation would seriously harm the one to whom we are making amends. We cannot, for example, unload a detailed account of a murderous gunfight or armed robbery upon the shoulders of our unsuspecting community or law enforcement. And even in those cases where such a matter must be discussed, let's try to avoid harming third parties, whoever they may be. It does not lighten our burden when we recklessly make the crosses of others heavier.

Many a razor-edged question can arise in other departments of life where this same principle is involved. Suppose, for instance, that we have stolen merchandise on the job, whether by arming ourselves or on heavily padding an expense account. Suppose that this may continue to go undetected if we say nothing. Do we instantly confess our irregularities to the company, in the practical certainty that we will be fired and become unemployable? Are we going to be so rigidly righteous about making amends that we don't care what happens to our family and home? Or do we first consult those who are to be gravely affected? Do we lay the matter before our sponsor or spiritual adviser, earnestly asking for God's help and guidance meanwhile resolving to do the right thing when it becomes clear, whatever the cost? Of course, there is no pat answer which can fit all such dilemmas. But all of them do require a complete willingness to make amends as fast and as far as may be possible in a given set of conditions. Above all, we should try to be absolutely sure that we are not delaying because we are afraid. For the readiness to take the full consequences of our past acts, and to take on responsibility for the wellbeing of others at the same time is the very spirit of Step Nine.

STEP TEN

"We continued to take personal inventory and when we admitted it."

Step Ten frees us from the wreckage of our present. If we do not stay aware of our defects, they can drive us into a corner that we cannot get out of crime free. One of the first things we learn in Gangsters Anonymous is that if we break the law, we lose. For the same reason, we will not experience as much pain if we can avoid the things that cause us pain. We continue to take a personal inventory and we form a habit of looking at ourselves, our actions, attitudes and relationships on a regular basis. We are creatures of habit and are vulnerable to our old ways of thinking and reacting. At times, it seems easier to continue in the old rut of self-destruction than to attempt a new and seemingly dangerous route. We do not have to be trapped by our old patterns. Today, we have a choice. The Tenth Step can help us correct our living problems and prevent their recurrence. We examine our actions during the day. Some of us write about our feelings explaining how we felt and what part we might have played in any problems, which occurred. Did we cause someone harm? Do we need to admit that we were wrong? If we find difficulties, we make an effort to take care of them. When these things are left undone, they have a way of festering.

This step can be a defense against the old insanity. We can ask ourselves if we are being drawn into old patterns of anger, resentment or fear. Do we feel trapped? Are we setting ourselves up for trouble? Are we too hungry, angry, lonely or tired? Are we taking ourselves too seriously? Are we judging our insides by the outside appearances of others? Do we suffer from some physical problem? The answers to these questions can help us deal with the difficulties of the moment. We no longer have to live with the feeling that we have a "hole in the gut". A lot of our chief concerns and major difficulties come from our inexperience with living without a gangsters' mentality. Often when we ask an old-timer what to do, we are amazed at the simplicity of the answer. The Tenth Step can be a pressure relief valve. We work this step while the day's difficulties are still fresh in our minds. We list what we have done and try not to rationalize our actions. This may be done in writing at the end of the day. The first thing we do is stop! Then we take the time to allow ourselves the privilege of thinking. We examine our actions, reactions, and motives. We often find that we have been doing better than we have been feeling. This allows us to examine our actions and admit fault, before things get any worse. We need to avoid rationalizing. We need to promptly admit our faults, not explain them.

We work this step continuously. This is a preventive action. The more we work this step the less we will need the corrective part of this step. This step is a great tool for avoiding grief before we bring it on ourselves. We monitor our feelings, emotions, fantasies and actions. By constantly looking at ourselves, we are able to avoid repeating the actions that make us feel bad. We need this step even when we are feeling good and when things are going well. Good feelings are new to us, and we need to nurture them. In times of trouble, we can try the things that worked during the good times. We have the right to feel good. We have a choice. The good times can also be a trap; the danger is that we may forget that our first priority is to stay crime free. For us, recovery is more than just pleasure.

We need to remember that everyone makes mistakes. We will never be perfect. However, we can accept ourselves by using Step Ten. By continuing a personal inventory, we are set free, in the here and now, from the past and ourselves. We no longer justify our existence. This step allows us to be ourselves. When we work the first nine steps, we prepare ourselves for the adventure of a new life. But when we approach Step Ten we commence to put our G.A. way of living to practical use, day by day, in foul weather or fair. Then comes the acid test: can we stay crime free, keep in emotional balance, and live to good purpose under all conditions?

A continuous look at our assets and liabilities, and a real desire to learn and grow by this means, are necessities for us. We recovering gangsters have learned this the hard way. More experienced people, of course, in all times and places have practiced unsparing self survey and criticism. For the wise have always known that no one can make much of his life until self searching becomes a regular habit, until he is able to admit and accept what he finds, and until he patiently and persistently tries to correct what is wrong.

When a member of the fellowship has a terrific hangover because he committed crimes the day before, he cannot live well today. But there is another kind of hangover, which; we all experience whether we are committing crimes or not. That is the emotional hangover, the direct result of yesterday's and sometimes today's excesses of negative emotion anger, fear, jealousy, and the like. If we want to live serenely today and tomorrow, we certainly need to eliminate these hangovers. This doesn't mean we need to wander morbidly around in the past. It requires an admission and correction of errors now. Our inventory enables us to settle with the past. When this is done, we are really able to leave it behind us. When our inventory is carefully taken, and we have made peace with ourselves, the conviction follows that tomorrow's challenges can be met as they come.

Although all inventories are alike in principle, the time factor does distinguish one from another. There's the spot-check inventory, taken at any time of the day, whenever we find ourselves getting tangled up. There's the one we take at day's end, when we review the happenings of the hours just past. Here we cast up a balance sheet, crediting ourselves with things well done, and chalking up debits where due. Then there are those occasions when alone, or in the company of our sponsor or spiritual adviser, we make a careful review of our progress since the last time we completed an inventory. Many members go in for annual or semiannual house cleanings. Many of us also like the experience of an occasional retreat from the outside world where we can quiet down for an undisturbed day or so of self overhaul and meditation.

Aren't these practices joy killers as well as time consumers? Must crime free members spend most of their waking hours drearily rehashing their sins of omission or commission? Well, hardly. The emphasis on inventory is heavy only because a great many of us have never really acquired the habit of accurate self appraisal. Once this healthy practice has become ingrained, it will be so interesting and profitable to see that the time it takes won't be missed. For these minutes and sometimes hours spent in self examination are bound to make all the other hours of our day better and happier. And at length our inventories become a regular part of everyday living, rather than something unusual or set apart.

Before we ask what a spot check inventory is, let's look at the kind of setting in which such an inventory can do its work. It is a spiritual saying that every time we are disturbed, no matter what the cause, there is something wrong with us. If somebody hurts us and we are sore, we are in the wrong also. But are there no exceptions to this rule? What about "justifiable" anger? If somebody cheats us, aren't we entitled to be mad? Can't we be properly angry with self-righteous folk? For crime free members of G.A. these are dangerous exceptions. We have found that justified anger ought to be left to those better qualified to handle it.

Few people have been more victimized by resentments than we recovering gangsters. It mattered little whether our resentments were justified or not. A burst of temper could spoil a day, and a well nursed grudge could make us miserably ineffective. Nor were we ever skillful in separating justified from unjustified anger. As we saw it, our wrath was always justified. Anger, that occasional luxury of more balanced people, could keep us on an emotional jag indefinitely. These emotional "crime free benders" often led straight to the bottle. Other kinds of disturbances, jealousy, envy, self-pity, or hurt pride, did the same thing.

A spot-check inventory taken in the midst of such disturbances can be of very great help in quieting stormy emotions. A daily spot check finds its chief purpose to situations which arise in our everyday march. The consideration of longstanding difficulties had better be postponed, when possible, to times deliberately set aside for that purpose. The quick inventory is aimed at our daily ups and downs, especially those where people or new events throw us off balance and tempt us to make mistakes. In all these situations we need self-restraint, honest analysis of what is involved, a willingness to admit when the fault is ours, and an equal willingness to forgive when the fault is elsewhere. We need not be discouraged when we fall into the error of our old ways, for these disciplines are not easy. We shall look for growth, not for perfection.

Our first objective will be the development of self-restraint. This carries a top priority rating. When we speak or act hastily or rashly, the ability to be fair-minded and tolerant evaporates on the spot. One unkind outburst or one willful snap judgment can ruin our relations with another person for a whole day, or maybe a whole year. Nothing pays off like restraint of tongue and pen. We must avoid quick-tempered criticism and furious, power driven argument. The same goes for sulking or silent scorn. These are emotional booby traps baited with pride and vengefulness. Our first job is to sidestep the traps. When we are tempted by the bait, we should train ourselves to step back and think. For we can neither think nor act in good purpose until the habit of self-restraint has become automatic.

Disagreeable or unexpected problems are not the only ones that call for self-control. We must be quite as careful when we begin to achieve some measure of importance and material success. For no one has ever loved personal triumphs more than we have loved them; we committed crimes successfully like a smooth wine which could never fail to make us feel elated. When temporary good fortune came our way, we indulged ourselves in fantasies of still greater victories over people and circumstances. Thus blinded by prideful self-confidence, we were apt to play the big shot. Of course, people turned away from us, bored or hurt. Now that we're in G.A. and crime free, and winning back the esteem of our friends and business associates, we find that we still need to exercise special vigilance. As an insurance against "big shotism" we can often check ourselves by remembering that we are today crime free only by the grace of God and that any success we may be having is far more His success than ours. Finally, we begin to see that all people, including ourselves, are to some extent emotionally ill as well as frequently wrong, and then we approach true tolerance and see what real love for our fellows actually means. It will become more and more evident as we go forward that it is pointless to become angry, or to get hurt by people who, like us, are suffering from the pains of growing up.

Such a radical change in our outlook will take time, maybe a lot of time. Not many people can truthfully assert that they love everybody. Most of us must admit that we have loved but a few; that we have been quite indifferent to many, so long as none of them gave us trouble; and as for the remainder, well, we have really disliked or hated them. Although these attitudes are common enough, we crime free members find we need something much better in order to keep our balance. We can't stand it if we hate deeply. The idea that we can be possessively loving of a few, can ignore the many, and can continue to fear or hate anybody, has to be abandoned, if only a little at a time.

We can try to stop making unreasonable demands upon those we love. We can show kindness where we had shown none. With those we dislike we can begin to practice justice and courtesy, perhaps going out of our way to understand and help them. Whenever we fail any of these people, we must promptly admit it to ourselves always, and to them also, when the admission would be helpful. Courtesy, kindness, justice, and love are the keynotes by which we may come into harmony with practically anybody. When in doubt we can always pause, saying, "Not my will, but Thy will, be done." And we can often ask ourselves, "Am I doing to others as I would have them do to me today?" When evening comes, perhaps just before going to sleep, many of us draw up a balance sheet for the day. This is a good place to remember that inventory taking is not always done in red ink. It's a poor day indeed when we haven't done something right. As a matter of fact, the waking hours are usually well filled with things that are constructive. Good intentions, good thoughts, and good acts are there for us to see. Even when we have tried hard and failed, we may chalk that up as one of the greatest credits of all. Under these conditions, the pains of failure are converted into assets. Out of them we receive the stimulation we need to go forward. Someone who knew what he was talking about once remarked that pain was the touchstone of all spiritual progress. How heartily we crime free members can agree with him, for we know that the pains of committing crimes had to come before crime free living, and emotional disorder before serenity.   Although we all wish we would have never committed the crime or crimes from the very beginning.

As we glance down the debit side of the day's ledger, we should carefully examine our motives in each thought or act that appears to be wrong. In most cases our motives won't be hard to see and understand. When prideful, angry, jealous, anxious, or fearful, we acted accordingly, and that was that. Here we need only recognize that we did act or think badly, try to visualize how we might have done better, and resolve with God's help to carry these lessons over into tomorrow, making, of course, any amends still neglected. But in other instances only the closest scrutiny will reveal what our true motives were. There are cases where our ancient enemy, rationalization, has stepped in and has justified conduct which was really wrong. The temptation here is to imagine that we had good motives and reasons when we really didn't. We "constructively criticized" someone who needed it, when our real motive was to win a useless argument. Or, the person concerned not being present, we thought we were helping others to understand him, when in actuality our true motive was to feel superior by pulling him down. We sometimes hurt those we love because they need to be "taught a lesson," when we really want to punish. We were depressed and complained we felt bad, when in fact we were mainly asking for sympathy and attention. This odd trait of mind and emotion, this perverse wish to hide a bad motive underneath a good one, permeates human affairs from top to bottom. This subtle and elusive kind of self–righteousness can underlie the smallest act or thought. Learning daily to spot, admit, and correct these flaws is the essence of character building and good living. An honest regret for harms done, a genuine gratitude for blessings received, and a willingness to try for better things tomorrow will be the permanent assets we shall seek. Having so considered our day, not omitting to take due note of things well done, and having searched our hearts with neither fear nor favor, we can truly thank God for the blessings we have received and sleep in good conscience.

STEP ELEVEN

"We sought through prayer and meditation to improve our conscious contact with God as we understood Him, praying only for knowledge of His will for us and the Power to carry that out."

The first ten steps have set the stage for us to improve our conscious contact with the God of our understanding. They gave us the foundation to achieve our long sought, positive goals. Having entered this phase of our spiritual program through practicing the previous steps, most of us welcome the exercise of prayer and meditation. Our spiritual condition is the basis for a successful recovery that offers unlimited growth. Many of us really begin to appreciate our recovery when we get to the Eleventh Step. In the Eleventh Step, our life takes on a deeper meaning. By surrendering control, we gain a far greater power. The nature of our belief will determine the manner of our prayers and meditations. We need only make sure that we have a system of belief that works for us. Results count in recovery. As has been noted elsewhere, our prayers seemed to work as soon as we entered the program of Gangsters Anonymous and we surrendered to our illness. The conscious contact described in this step is the direct result of living the steps. We use this step to improve and maintain our spiritual condition.

When we first came into the program, we received

help from a Power greater than ourselves. This was set in motion by our surrender to the program. The purpose of the Eleventh Step is to increase our awareness of that power and to improve our ability to use it as a source of strength in our new life. The more we improve our conscious contact with our God through prayer and meditation the easier it is to say, "Your will, not mine, be done." We can ask for God's help when we need it, and our life get better. The experiences that some people talk about regarding meditation and individual religious beliefs do not always apply to us. Ours is a spiritual, not religious, program.

By the time we get to the Eleventh Step, character defects that caused our problems in the past have been addressed by working the preceding ten steps. The image of the kind of person that we would like to be is a long look at God's will for us. Often our outlook is so limited that we can only see our immediate wants and needs. It is easy to slip back into our old ways. To insure our continued growth and recovery, we have to learn to maintain our life on a spiritually sound base. God will not force his goodness on us, but we will receive it if we ask. We usually feel something is different in the moment, but do not see the change in our life until later. When we finally get our own selfish motives out of the way, we begin to find a peace that we never imagined possible. Enforced morality lacks the power that comes to us when we choose to live a spiritual life. Most of us pray when we are hurting. We learn that if we pray regularly we will not be hurting as often, or as intensely.

Outside of Gangsters Anonymous, there are a number of different groups practicing meditation. Nearly all of these groups are connected with a particular religion or philosophy. An endorsement of any of these methods would be a violation of our traditions and a restriction on the individual's right to have a God of his understanding. Meditation allows us to develop spiritually in our own way. Some of the things that did not work for us in the past might work today. We take a fresh look at each day with an open mind. We know that if we pray for God's will, we will receive what is best for us, regardless of what we think. This knowledge is based on our beliefs and experience as recovering gangsters. Prayer is communicating our concerns to a power greater than ourselves. Sometimes when we pray, a remarkable thing happens; we find the means, ways and energies to perform tasks far beyond our capabilities. We grasp the limitless strength provided for us through our daily prayer and surrender, as long as we keep the faith and renew it.

Prayer is asking for God's help; meditation is listening for God's answer. We learn to be careful of praying for specific things. We pray that God will show us his will, and that He will help us carry that out. In some cases, he makes His will so obvious to us that we have little difficulty seeing it. In others, our egos are so self-centered that we will not accept God's will for us without struggle and surrender. If we pray for God to remove any distracting influences, the quality of our prayers usually improves and we feel the difference. Prayer takes practice, and we should remind ourselves that skilled people were not born with their skills. It took lots of effort on their part to develop them. Through prayer, we seek conscious contact with our God. In meditation, we achieve this contact, and the Eleventh Step helps us to maintain it.

We may have been exposed to many religions and meditative disciplines before coming to Gangsters Anonymous. Some of us were devastated and completely confused by these practices. We were sure that it was God's will for us to live life as gangsters to reach higher consciousness. We fell into the theory that we must protect ourselves; loved ones, and cultures to the last of our breaths. We did not understand that God is there and has our backs through all of life difficulties. We lost faith in some who are paid to protect and serve. Many of us found ourselves in very strange states because of these practices. We never suspected the damaging effects of some mentors, some parents, and some community leaders had on our psyche. A root of our difficulties and pursued to the end.

In quiet moments of meditation, God's will become evident to us. Quieting the mind through meditation brings an inner peace that brings us into contact with the God within us. A basic premise of meditation is that it is difficult, if not impossible, to obtain conscious contact unless our mind is still. The usual, never-ending succession of thoughts has to cease for progress to be made. Therefore, our preliminary practice is aimed at stilling the mind, and letting the thoughts that arise die a natural death. We leave our thoughts behind, as the meditation part of the Eleventh step becomes a reality for us. Emotional balance is one of the first results of meditation, and our experience bears this out. Some of us came into the program broken, and hung around for a while, only to find God or salvation in one kind of religious cult or another. It is easy to float back out the door on a cloud of religious zeal and forget that we are gangsters with an incurable desire to create havoc.

It is said that for meditation to be of value, the results must show in our daily life. This fact is implicit in the Eleventh Step: "His will for us and the power to carry that out", for those of us who do not pray, meditation is our only way of working this step. We find ourselves praying because it brings us peace and restores confidence and courage. It helps us to live a life that is free of fear and distrust. When we remove our selfish motives and pray for guidance, we find feelings of peace and serenity. We begin to experience awareness and an empathy with other people that was not possible before working this step. As we seek our personal contact with God, we begin to open up as a flower in the sun. We begin to see that God's love has been present all the time, just waiting for us to accept it. We do the footwork and accept freedom happily on a daily basis. We find relying on God becomes more comfortable for us.

When we first come to the program, we usually ask for many things that seem to be important, our wants and needs. As we grow spiritually and find a higher power greater than ourselves, we find we begin to realize that as long as our spiritual needs are met, our living problems are reduced to a point of comfort. When we forget where our real strength lies, we quickly become subject to the patterns of thinking and action that got us into the program in the first place. We eventually redefine our beliefs and understanding to the point where we see that our greatest need is for knowledge of God's will for us and the strength to perform his will. We are able to set aside some of our personal preferences, because we learn that God's will for us becomes our own true will for ourselves. This happens in an intuitive manner, no explanation needed.

We become willing to let other people be who they are without having to pass judgment on them. The urgency to take care of things is not there anymore. We could not comprehend acceptance in the beginning; today we can. We know that whatever the day brings, God has given us everything we need for our spiritual well-being. It is all right for us to admit powerlessness, because God is powerful enough to help us stay clean and to enjoy spiritual progress. God is helping us to get our house in order.

We begin to see more clearly what is real. Through constant contact with our Higher Power, the answers that we seek come to us. We gain the ability to do what we once could not. We respect the beliefs of others. We encourage you to seek strength and guidance according to your belief. We are thankful for this step, because we begin to get what is best for us. We prayed for our wants and once we got them, we felt trapped. We could pray and get something, then have to pray for its removal, because we could not handle it.

The members of Gangsters Anonymous hope that having learned the power of prayer and the responsibility prayer brings with it, we can use the Eleventh Step as a guideline for our daily program. We begin to pray for God's will for us. This way we are getting only what we are capable of handling. We are able to respond to it and handle it, because God helps us prepare for it. Some of us simply use our words to give thanks for God's grace.

In an attitude of surrender and humility, we approach this step repeatedly to receive the gift of knowledge and strength from the God of our understanding. The Tenth Step clears away the errors of the present so we may work the Eleventh Step. Without this step, it is unlikely that we could experience a spiritual awakening, practice spiritual principles in our life or carry a sufficient message to attract others to recovery. In order to keep it, there is a spiritual principle of giving away what you learn in Gangsters Anonymous. By helping others stay crime free, we enjoy the benefit of the spiritual wealth that we have found. We must give freely and gratefully that which has been freely and gratefully given to us. Prayer and meditation are our principal means of conscious contact with God.

We crime free members of G.A. are active folk, enjoying the satisfactions of dealing with the realities of life, usually for the first time in our life, and strenuously trying to help the next thug life individual who comes along. So it isn't surprising that we often tend to slight serious meditation and prayer as something not really necessary. To be sure, we feel it is something that might help us to meet an occasional emergency, but at first many of us are apt to regard it as a somewhat mysterious skill of clergymen, from which we may hope to get a secondhand benefit. Or perhaps we don't believe in these things at all.

To certain newcomers and to those onetime agnostics who still cling to G.A. as their higher power, we hope you find the power of prayer, despite all the logic and experience in proof of it, still be unconvincing or quite objectionable. Those of us who once felt this way can certainly understand and sympathize. We well remember how something deep inside us kept rebelling against the idea of bowing before any God. Many of us had strong logic, too, which "proved" there was no God whatsoever. What about all the accidents, sickness, cruelty, and injustice in the world? What about all those unhappy life which were the direct result of unfortunate birth situations and uncontrollable circumstances? Surely there could be no justice in this scheme of things, and therefore no God at all.

Sometimes we took a slightly different tack. Sure, we said to ourselves, the hen probably did come before the egg. No doubt the universe had a "first cause" of some sort, the God of the Atom, maybe, hot and cold by turns. But certainly there wasn't any evidence of a God who knew or cared about human beings. We liked G.A. all right, and were quick to say that it had done miracles. But we recoiled from meditation and prayer as obstinately as the scientist who refused to perform a certain experiment lest it prove his pet theory wrong. Of course we finally did experiment, and when unexpected results followed, we felt different; in fact we knew different and so we were sold on meditation and prayer. And that, we have found, can happen to anybody who tries. It has been well said that "almost the only scoffers at prayer are those who never tried it enough."

Those of us who have come to make regular use of prayer would no more do without it than we would refuse air, food, or sunshine. And for the same reason. When we refuse air, light, or food, the body suffers. And when we turn away from meditation and prayer, we likewise deprive our minds, our emotions, and our intuitions of vitally needed support. As the body can fail its purpose from lack of nourishment, so can the soul. We all need the light of God's reality, the nourishment of His strength, and the atmosphere of His grace. To an amazing extent the facts of crime free living confirm this ageless truth.

There is a direct linkage among self–examination, meditation, and prayer. Taken separately, these practices can bring much relief and benefit. But when they are logically related and interwoven, the result is an unshakable foundation for life. Now and then we may be granted a glimpse of that ultimate reality which is God's kingdom. And we will be comforted and assured that our own destiny in that realm will be secure for so long as we try, however falteringly, to find and do the will of our own Creator.

As we have seen, self searching is the means by which we bring new vision, action, and grace to bear upon the dark and negative side of our natures. It is a step in the development of that kind of humility that makes it possible for us to receive God's help. Yet it is only a step. We will want to go further. We will want the good that is in us all, even in the worst of us, to flower and to grow. Most certainly we shall need bracing air and an abundance of food. But first of all we shall want sunlight; nothing much can grow in the dark. Meditation is our step out into the sun. How, then, shall we meditate?

The actual experience of meditation and prayer across the centuries is, of course, immense. The world's libraries and places of worship are a treasure trove for all seekers. It is to be hoped that every crime free member of Gangsters Anonymous who has a religious connection which emphasizes meditation will return to the practice of that devotion as never before. But what about the rest of us who are less fortunate don't know how to begin? Well, we might start like this. First let's look at a really good prayer. We won't have far to seek; the great men and women of all religions have left us a wonderful supply. Here let us consider one that is a classic. Its author was a man who for several hundred years now has been rated as a saint. We won't be biased or scared off by that fact, because although he was not a recovering gangster he did, like us, go through the emotional wringer. And as he came out the other side of that painful experience, this prayer was his expression of what he could then see, feel, and wish to become:

"Lord, make me a channel of thy peace that where there is hatred, I may bring love, that where there is wrong, I may bring the spirit of forgiveness, that where there is discord, I may bring harmony, that where there is error, I may bring truth, that where there is doubt, I may bring faith, that where there is despair, I may bring hope, that where there are shadows, I may bring light, that where there is sadness, I may bring joy. Lord, grant that I may seek to comfort rather than to be comforted, to understand, than to be understood, to love, than to be loved. For it is by self forgetting that one finds it, is by forgiving that one is forgiven. It is by dying that one awakens to Eternal Life. Amen." As beginners in meditation, we might now reread this prayer several times very slowly, savoring every word and trying to take in the deep meaning of each phrase and idea. It will help if we can drop all resistance to what our friend says. For in meditation, debate has no place. We rest quietly with the thoughts of someone who knows, so that we may experience and learn.

As though lying upon a sunlit beach, let us relax and breathe deeply of the spiritual atmosphere with which the grace of this prayer surrounds us. Let us become willing to partake and be strengthened and lifted up by the sheer spiritual power, beauty, and love of which these magnificent words are the carriers. Let us look now upon the sea and ponder what its mystery is; and let us lift our eyes to the far horizon, beyond which we shall seek all those wonders still unseen. "Shucks!" says somebody. "This is nonsense. It isn't practical."

When such thoughts break in, we might recall, a little regretfully, how much drama we used to set off, with imagination as we tried to create reality out of criminal behavior. Yes, we reveled in that sort of thinking, didn't we? And though crime free nowadays, we don't often try to do much the same thing? Perhaps our trouble was not that we used our imagination. Perhaps the real trouble was our almost total inability to point our imaginations toward the right objectives. There's nothing wrong with constructive imagination; all sound achievement rests upon it. After all, no man can build a house until he first envisions a plan for it. Well, meditation is like that, too; it helps to envision our spiritual objective before we try to move toward it. So let's get back to that sunlit beach or to the plains or to the mountains, if you prefer.

When, by such simple devices, we have placed ourselves in a mood in which we can focus undisturbed on constructive imagination, we might proceed like this: Once more we read our prayer, and again try to see what its inner essence is. We'll think now about the man who first uttered the prayer. First of all, he wanted to become a "channel." Then he asked for the grace to bring love, forgiveness, harmony, truth, faith, hope, light, and joy to every human being he could.

Next came the expression of an aspiration and a hope for himself. He hoped, God willing, that he might be able to find some of these treasures, too. This he would try to do by what he called self forgetting. What did he mean by "self forgetting," and how did he propose to accomplish that? He thought it better to give comfort than to receive it; better to understand than to be understood; better to forgive than to be forgiven. This much could be a fragment of what is called meditation, perhaps our very first attempt at a mood, a channel into the realm of spirit, if you like. It ought to be followed by a good look at where we stand now, and a further look at what might happen in our life were we able to move closer to the ideal we have been trying to glimpse. Meditation is something which can always be further developed. It has no boundaries, either of width or height. Aided by such instruction and example as we can find, it is essentially an individual adventure, something which each one of us works out in his own way. But its objective is always the same: to improve our conscious contact with God, with His grace, wisdom, and love. And let's always remember that meditation is in reality intensely practical. One of its first fruits is emotional balance. With it we can broaden and deepen the channel between ourselves and God as we understand Him.

Now, what of prayer? Prayer is the raising of the heart and mind to God and in this sense it includes meditation. How may we go about it? And how does it fit in with meditation? Prayer, as commonly understood, is a petition to God. Having opened our channel as best we can, we try to ask for those right things of which we and others are in the greatest need. And we think that the whole range of our needs is well defined by that part of Step Eleven which says: "... knowledge of His will for us and the power to carry that out." A request for this fits in any part of our day.

In the morning we think of the hours to come. Perhaps we think of our day's work and the chances it may afford us to be useful and helpful, or of some special problem that it may bring. Possibly today will see a continuation of a serious and as yet unresolved problem left over from yesterday. Our immediate temptation will be to ask for specific solutions to specific problems, and for the ability to help other people as we have already thought they should be helped. In that case, we are asking God to do it our way. Therefore, we ought to consider each request carefully to see what its real merit is. Even so, when making specific requests, it would do well to add to each one of them this qualification: ". . . if it be Thy will." We ask simply that throughout the day God place in us the best understanding of His will that we can have for that day, and that we be given the grace by which we may carry it out.

As the day goes on, we can pause where situations must be met and decisions made, and renew the simple request: "Thy will, not mine, be done." If at these points our emotional disturbance happens to be great, we will most surely keep our balance, provided we remember, and repeat to ourselves, a particular prayer or phrase that has appealed to us in our reading or meditation. Just saying it over and over will often enable us to clear a channel choked up with anger, fear, frustration, or misunderstanding, and permit us to return to our search for God's will, not our own, in the moment of stress. At these critical moments, if we remind ourselves that "it is better to comfort than to be comforted, to understand than to be understood, to love than to be loved," we will be following the intent of Step Eleven.

Of course, it is reasonable and understandable that the question is asked often: "Why can't we take a specific and troubling dilemma straight to God, and in prayer secure from Him sure and definite answers to our requests?" This can be done, but it has hazards. We have seen crime free members ask with much earnestness and faith for God's explicit guidance on matters ranging all the way from a shattering domestic or financial crisis to correcting a minor personal fault, like being late for work. Quite often, however, the thoughts that seem to come from God are not answers at all. They prove to be well intentioned unconscious rationalizations. The G.A., or indeed any man, who tries to run his life rigidly by this kind of prayer, by this self serving demand of God for replies, is a particularly disconcerting individual. To any questioning or criticism of his actions he instantly proffers his reliance upon prayer for guidance in all matters great or small. He may have forgotten the possibility that his own wishful thinking and the human tendency to rationalize have distorted his so-called guidance. With the best of intentions, he tends to force his own will into all sorts of situations and problems with the comfortable assurance that he is acting under God's specific direction. Under such an illusion, he can of course create great havoc without in the least intending it.

We also fall into another similar temptation. We form ideas as to what we think God's will is for other people. We say to ourselves, "This one ought to be cured of his fatal malady," or "That one ought to be relieved of his emotional pain," and we pray for these specific things. Such prayers, of course, are fundamentally good acts, but often they are based upon a supposition that we know God's will for the person for whom we pray. This means that side by side with an earnest prayer there can be a certain amount of presumption and conceit in us. It is crime free members experience that particularly in these cases we ought to pray that God's will, whatever it is, be done for others as well as for ourselves.

In G.A. we have found that the actual good results of prayer are beyond question. They are matters of knowledge and experience. All those who have persisted have found strength not ordinarily their own. They have found wisdom beyond their usual capability. And they have increasingly found a peace of mind which can stand firm in the face of difficult circumstances.

We discover that we do receive guidance for our life to just about the extent that we stop making demands upon God to give it to us on order and on our terms. Almost any experienced crime free member of G.A. will tell how his affairs have taken remarkable and unexpected turns for the better as he tried to improve his conscious contact with God. He will also report that out of every season of grief or suffering, when the hand of God seemed heavy or even unjust, new lessons for living were learned, new resources of courage were uncovered, and that finally, inescapably, the conviction came that God does "move in a mysterious way His wonders to perform."

All this should be very encouraging news for those who recoil from prayer because they don't believe in it, or because they feel themselves cut off from God's help and direction. All of us, without exception, pass through times when we can pray only with the greatest exertion of will. Occasionally we go even further than this. We are seized with a rebellion so sickening that we simply won't pray. When these things happen we should not think too ill of ourselves. We should simply resume prayer as soon as we can, doing what we know to be good for us. Perhaps one of the greatest rewards of meditation and prayer is the sense of belonging that comes to us. We no longer live in a completely hostile world. We are no longer lost and frightened and purposeless. The moment we catch even a glimpse of God's will, the moment we begin to see truth, justice, and love as the real and eternal things in life, we are no longer deeply disturbed by all the seeming evidence to the contrary that surrounds us in purely human affairs. We know that God lovingly watches over us. We know that when we turn to Him, all will be well with us, here and hereafter.

STEP TWELVE

"Having had a spiritual awakening as a result of these steps, we tried to carry this message to still suffering gangsters, and to practice these principles in all our affairs."

We came to Gangsters Anonymous as the result of the wreckage of our past. The last thing we expected was an awakening of the spirit. We just wanted to stop hurting. All of the steps lead to an awakening of a spiritual nature. This awakening is evidenced by changes in our life. These changes make us better able to live by spiritual principles and to carry our message of recovery and hope to the addict who still suffers. The message, however, is meaningless unless we live it. As we live it, our life and actions give more meaning than our words and literature ever could. The idea of a spiritual awakening takes many different forms in the different personalities that we find in the fellowship. However, all spiritual awakenings have some things in common. Common elements include an end to loneliness and a sense of direction in our life. Many of us believe that a spiritual awakening is meaningless unless accompanied by an increase in peace of mind and concern for others. In order to maintain peace of mind, we strive to live in the here and now. Those of us who have worked these steps to the best of our ability received many benefits. We believe that these benefits are a direct result of living this program. When we first begin to enjoy relief from our gangster mentality, we run the risk of assuming to control of our life again. We forget the agony and pain that we have known. Our illness controlled our life when we used a gangsters' mentality. It is ready and waiting to take over again. We quickly forgot that all our past efforts at controlling our life failed. By this time, most of us realize that the only way that we can keep what was given to us is by sharing this new gift of life with the still-suffering person within this gangsters mentality. This is our best insurance against relapse to the torturous existence of living life gangster. We call it carrying the message, and we do it in a number of ways. In the Twelfth Step, we practice the spiritual principles of giving the G.A. message of recovery in order to keep it. Even a member with one day in the G. A. fellowship can carry the message that this program works.

When we share with someone new, we are used as a spiritual instrument of our Higher Power. We do not set ourselves up as gods. We often ask for help of another recovering gangster when sharing with a new comer. It is a privilege to respond to a cry for help. We, who have been in the pits of despair, feel fortunate to help others find recovery. We help new people learn the principles of Gangsters Anonymous. We try to make them feel welcome and help them learn what the program has to offer. We share our experience, strength and hope. Whenever possible, we accompany newcomers to a meeting. The selfless service of this work is the very principle of Step Twelve. We received our recovery from the God of our understanding. We now make ourselves available as His tool to share recovery with those who seek it. Most of us learn that we can only carry the message to someone who is asking for help. Sometimes the only message necessary to make the suffering gangster reach out is the power of example. A gangster may be suffering and be unwilling to ask for help. We can make ourselves available to these people, so when they ask, someone will be there.

Learning to help others is a benefit of the Gangsters Anonymous Program. Remarkably, working the twelve steps guides us from humiliation and despair to acting as instruments of our Higher Power. We are given the ability to help a fellow gangster when no one else can. We see it happening among us every day. This miraculous turnabout is evidence of a spiritual awakening. We share from our own personal experience what it has been like for us. The temptation to give advice is great, but when we do so, we lose the respect of newcomers. This clouds our message. A simple, honest message of recovery from our gangsters mentality rings true. We attend meetings and make ourselves visible and available to serve the Fellowship. We give freely and gratefully of our time, service, and what we have found here. The service we speak of in Gangsters Anonymous is the primary purpose of our group. Service work is carrying the message to the gangster who still suffers. The more eagerly we wade in and work, the richer our spiritual awakening will *be.* The first way we carry the message speaks for itself. People see us on the street and remember us as devious, frightened loners. They notice the fear leaving our faces. They see us gradually come alive.

Once we find G.A., boredom and complacency have no place in our new life. By staying crime-free, we begin to practice spiritual principles such as hope, surrender, acceptance, honesty, open-mindedness, willingness, faith, tolerance, patience, humility, unconditional love, sharing and caring. As our recovery progresses, spiritual principles touch every area of our life, because we simply try to live this program in the here and now. We find joy as we start to learn how to live by the principles of recovery. It is the joy of watching what a person two days crime-free says to a person with one day crime-free. A gangster alone is in bad company; it is the joy of watching a person who was struggling to make it, suddenly in the middle of helping another gangster stay crime-free become able. We feel that our life have become worthwhile. Spiritually refreshed, we are glad to be alive. When we were solving our problems with a gangsters' mentality, our life became an exercise in survival. Now we are doing much more than just surviving we are living. Realizing that the bottom line is staying crime free, we can enjoy life. We like being crime free and enjoy carrying the message of recovery to the gangster who still suffers. Going to meetings really works.

Practicing spiritual principles in our daily life leads us to a new image of ourselves. Honesty, humility and open-mindedness help us to treat our associates fairly. Our decisions are filled with tolerance. We learn to respect ourselves. The lessons we learn in our recovery are sometimes bitter and painful. By helping others we find the reward of self-respect, as we are able to share these lessons with other members of Gangsters Anonymous. We cannot deny other gangsters their pain, but we can carry the message of hope that was given to us by fellow gangsters in recovery. We share the principles of recovery as they have worked in our life. God helps us as we help each other. Life takes on a new meaning, a new joy, and a quality of being and feeling worthwhile. We become spiritually refreshed and are glad to be alive. One aspect of our spiritual awakening comes through the new understanding of our Higher Power that we develop by sharing another gangster's recovery. Yes, we are a vision of hope. We are examples of the program working. The joy that we have in living crime-free is an attraction to the gangster who still suffers. We do recover to live crime free and happy life. Welcome to G.A.!! The steps do not end here. The steps are a new beginning! The joy of living is the theme of G.A.'s Twelfth Step, and action is its key word. Here we turn outward toward our fellow recovering gangsters who are still in distress. Here we experience the kind of giving that asks no rewards. Here we begin to practice all Twelve Steps of the program in our daily life so that we and those about us may find crime free living. When the Twelfth Step is seen in its full implication, it is really talking about the kind of love that has no price tag on it. Our Twelfth Step also says that as a result of practicing all the Steps, we have each found something called a spiritual awakening. To new crime free members this often seems like a very dubious and improbable state of affairs. "What do you mean when you talk about a 'spiritual awakening'?" they ask. Maybe there are as many definitions of spiritual awakening as there are people who have had them. But certainly each genuine one has something in common with all the others. And these things that they have in common are not too hard to understand. When a man or a woman has a spiritual awakening, the most important meaning of it is that they now become able to do, feel, and believe that they could not do before on their unaided strength and resources alone. He has been granted a gift which amounts to a new state of consciousness and being. He has been set on a path which tells him he is really going somewhere, that life is not a dead end, not something to be endured or mastered. In a very real sense he has been transformed, because he has laid hold of a source of strength that, in one way or another, he had hitherto denied himself. He finds himself in possession of a degree of honesty, tolerance, unselfishness, peace of mind, and love of which he had thought himself quite incapable. What he has received is a free gift, and yet usually, at least in some small part, he has made himself ready to receive it.

Crime free members manner of making ready to receive this gift lies in the practice of the Twelve Steps in our program. So let's consider briefly what we have been trying to do up to this point: Step One showed us an amazing paradox: We found that we were totally unable to be rid of the obsession until we first admitted that we were powerless over it. In Step Two we saw that since we could not restore ourselves to sanity, some Higher Power must necessarily do so if we were to survive. Consequently, in Step Three we turned our will and our life over to the care of God as we understood Him. For the time being, we who were atheist or agnostic discovered that our own group, or G.A. as a whole, would suffice as a higher power. Beginning with Step Four, we commenced to search out the things in ourselves which had brought us to physical, moral, and spiritual bankruptcy. We made a searching and fearless moral inventory. Looking at Step Five, we decided that an inventory, taken alone, wouldn't be enough. We knew we would have to quit the deadly business of living alone with our conflicts, and in honesty confide these to God and another human being. At Step Six, many of us balked for the practical reason that we did not wish to have all our defects of character removed, because we still loved some of them too much. Yet we knew we had to make a settlement with the fundamental principle of Step Six. So we decided that while we still had some flaws of character that we could not yet relinquish, we ought to nevertheless quit our stubborn, rebellious hanging on to them. We said to ourselves, "This I cannot do today, perhaps, but I can stop crying out 'No, never!' Then, in Step Seven, we humbly asked God to remove our shortcomings only as He could or would under the conditions of the day we asked. In Step Eight, we continued our housecleaning, for we saw that we were not only in conflict with ourselves, but also with people and situations in the world in which we lived. We had to begin to make our peace, and so we listed the people we had harmed and became willing to set things right. We followed this up in Step Nine by making direct amends to those concerned, except when it would injure them or other people. By this time, at Step Ten, we had begun to get a basis for daily living, and we keenly realized that we would need to continue taking personal inventory, and that when we were in the wrong we ought to admit it promptly. In Step Eleven we saw that if a Higher Power had restored us to sanity and had enabled us to live with some peace of mind in a sorely troubled world, then such a Higher Power was worth knowing better, by as direct contact as possible. The persistent use of meditation and prayer, we found, did open the channel so that where there had been a trickle, there now was a river which led to sure power and safe guidance from God as we were increasingly better able to understand Him.

So, in practicing these Steps, we had a spiritual awakening about which finally there was no question. Looking at those who were only beginning and still doubted themselves, the rest of us were able to see the change setting in. From great numbers of such experiences, we could predict that the doubter who still claimed that he hadn't got the "spiritual angle," and who still considered his well loved G.A. group the higher power, would presently love God and call Him by name.

Now, what about the rest of the Twelfth Step? The wonderful energy it releases and the eager action by which it carries our message to the next suffering recovering gangster and which finally translates the Twelve Steps into action upon all our affairs is the payoff, the magnificent reality, of Gangsters Anonymous. Newcomers find undreamed of rewards. He tries to help his brother recovering gangster, the one who is even blinder than he. This is indeed the kind of giving that actually demands nothing. He does not expect his brother sufferer to pay him, or even to love him. And then he discovers that by the divine paradox of this kind of giving he has found his own reward, whether his brother has yet received anything or not. His own character may still be gravely defective, but he somehow knows that God has enabled him to make a mighty beginning, and he senses that he stands at the edge of new mysteries, joys, and experiences of which he had never even dreamed.

Practically every G.A. member declares that no satisfaction has been deeper and no joy greater than in a Twelfth Step well done. To watch the eyes of men and women open with wonder as they move from darkness into light; to see their life quickly fill with new purpose and meaning; to see whole families reassembled; to see the recovering gangster that was an outcast received back into his community in full citizenship; and above all to watch these people awaken to the presence of a loving God in their life. These things are the substance of what we receive as we carry the crime free message to the next recovering gangster.

Nor is this the only kind of Twelfth Step work. We sit in G.A. meetings and listen, not only to receive something for ourselves, but to give the reassurance and support that our presence can bring. If our turn comes to speak at a meeting, we again try to carry the crime free message. Whether our audience is one or many, it is still Twelfth Step work. There are many opportunities even for those of us who feel unable to speak at meetings or who are so situated that we cannot do much face to face Twelfth Step work. We can be the ones who take on the unspectacular but important tasks that makes good Twelfth Step work possible, perhaps arranging for the coffee and cake after the meetings, where so many skeptical, suspicious newcomers have found confidence and comfort in the laughter and talk where they can relax their guard. This is Twelfth Step work in the very best sense of the word. "Freely ye have received; freely give" is the core of this part of Step Twelve. We may often pass through Twelfth Step experiences where we will seem to be temporarily off the beam. These will appear as big setbacks at the time, but will be seen later as stepping stones to better things. For example, we may set our hearts on getting a particular person crime freed up, and after doing all we can for months, we see him relapse. Perhaps this will happen in a succession of cases, and we may be deeply discouraged as to our ability to carry the crime free message. Or we may encounter the reverse situation, in which we are highly elated because we seem to have been successful. Here the temptation is to become rather possessive of these newcomers. Perhaps we try to give them advice about their affairs that we aren't really competent to give or ought not give at all. Then we are hurt and confused when the advice is rejected, or when it is accepted and brings still greater confusion. By doing a great deal of dedicated Twelfth Step work, we sometimes carry the message to so many recovering gangsters that they place us in a position of trust. They make us, let us say, the group's chairman. Here again we are presented with the temptation to over manage things, and sometimes this results in rebuffs and other consequences which are hard to take.

But in the long run we clearly realize that these are only the pains of growing up, and nothing but good can come from them if we turn more and more to the entire Twelve Steps for the answers. Now comes the biggest question yet. What about the practice of these principles in all our affairs? Can we love the whole pattern of living as eagerly as we do the small segment of it we discover when we try to help other gangsters achieve a crime free life? Can we bring the same spirit of love and tolerance into our sometimes deranged family life that we bring to our G.A. group? Can we have the same kind of confidence and faith in these people who have been infected and sometimes crippled by our own illness that we have in our sponsors? Can we actually carry the G.A. spirit into our daily work? Can we meet our newly recognized responsibilities to the world at large? And can we bring new purpose and devotion to the religion of our choice? Can we find a new joy of living in trying to do something about all these things?

Furthermore, how shall we come to terms with seemingly failure or success? Can we now accept and adjust to either without despair or pride? Can we accept poverty, sickness, loneliness, and bereavement with courage and serenity? Can we steadfastly content ourselves with the humbler, yet sometimes more durable, satisfactions when the brighter, more glittering achievements are denied us? The G.A. answer to these questions about living is: "Yes, all of these things are possible." We know this because we see monotony, pain, and even calamity turned to good use by those who keep on trying to practice crime free members Twelve Steps. And if these are facts of life for the many crime free individuals who have recovered in G.A., they can become the facts of life for many more.

Of course all crime free members, even the best, fall

far short of such achievements as a consistent thing. Without necessarily taking that first drink, we often get quite far off the beam. Our troubles sometimes begin with indifference. We are crime free and happy in our G.A. work. Things go well at home and the office. We naturally congratulate ourselves on what later proves to be a far too easy and superficial point of view. We temporarily cease to grow because we feel satisfied that there is no need for Twelve Step work for us. We are doing fine on a few of them. Maybe we are doing fine on only two of them, the First Step and that part of the Twelfth Step where we "carry the message." In G.A. slang, that blissful state is known as "two stepping." And it can go on for years.

The best intentioned of us can fall for the "two-step" illusion. Sooner or later the pink cloud stage wears off and things begin to be disappointingly dull. We begin to think that G.A. doesn't pay off after all. We become puzzled and discouraged. Then perhaps life, as it has a way of doing, suddenly hands us a great big lump that we can't begin to swallow, let alone digest. We fail to get a worked for promotion. We lose that good job. Maybe there are serious domestic or romantic difficulties, or perhaps that boy we thought God was looking after becomes a military casualty. What then? Have we crime free individuals in G.A. gotten, or can we get, the resources to meet these calamities that come to so many? These were problems of life which we could never face up to. Can we now, with the help of God as we understand Him, handle them as well and as bravely as our law abiding friends often do? Can we transform these calamities into assets, sources of growth and comfort to ourselves and those around us? Well, we surely have a chance if we switch from "two stepping" to "twelve stepping," if we are willing to receive that grace of God which can sustain and strengthen us in any catastrophe.

Our basic troubles are the same as everyone else's, but when an honest effort is made "to practice these principles in all our affairs," well grounded crime free members seem to have the ability, by God's grace, to take these troubles in stride and turn them into demonstrations of faith. We have seen crime free members suffer drawn out and fatal illnesses with little complaint, and often in good cheer. We have sometimes seen families broken apart by misunderstanding, tensions, or actual infidelity, who are reunited by the G.A. way of life. Though the earning power of most crime free members is relatively high, we have some members who never seem to get on their feet money wise, and still others who encounter heavy financial reverses. Ordinarily we see these situations met with fortitude and faith. Like most people, we have found that we can take our big lumps as they come. But also like others, we often discover a greater challenge in the lesser and more continuous problems of life. Our answer is in still more spiritual development. Only by this practice can we improve our chances for really happy and useful living. And as we grow spiritually, we find that our old attitudes toward our instincts need to undergo drastic revisions. Our desires for emotional security and wealth, for personal prestige and power, for romance, and for family satisfactions all these have to be tempered and redirected. We have learned that the satisfaction of our instincts cannot be the sole end and aim of our life. If we place instincts first, we have got the cart before the horse; we shall be pulled backward into disillusionment. But when we are willing to place spiritual growth first then, and only then, do we have a real chance.

After we come into G.A., if we continue growing, our attitudes and actions toward security, emotional security and financial security, commence to change profoundly. Our demand for emotional security, for our own way, had constantly thrown us into unworkable relations with other people. Though we were sometimes quite unconscious of this, the result always had been the same. Either we had tried to play God and dominate those around us, or we had insisted on being over dependent on them. Where people had temporarily let us run their life as though they were still children, we had felt very happy and secure. But when they finally resisted or ran away, we were bitterly hurt and disappointed. We blamed them, being quite unable to see that our unreasonable demands had been the cause.

When we had taken the opposite tack and had insisted, like infants ourselves, that people protect and take care of us or that the world owed us a living, then the result had been equally unfortunate. This often caused the people we had loved most to push us aside or perhaps desert us entirely. Our disillusionment had been hard to bear. We couldn't imagine people acting that way toward us. We had failed to see that though adult in years we were still behaving childishly, trying to turn everybody, friends, wives, husbands, even the world itself into protective parents. We had refused to learn the very hard lesson that over dependence on people is unsuccessful because all people are fallible, and even the best of them will sometimes let us down, especially when our demands for attention become unreasonable.

As we made spiritual progress, we saw through these lies. It became clear that if we ever were to feel emotionally secure among grownup people, we would have to live our life on a give and take basis; we would have to develop the sense of being in partnership or brotherhood with all those around us. We saw that need to give constantly of ourselves without demands for repayment. When we persistently did this we gradually found that people were attracted to us as never before. And even if they failed us, we could be understanding and not too seriously affected.

When we developed still more, we discovered the best possible source of emotional stability to be God Himself. We found that dependence upon His perfect justice, forgiveness, and love was healthy, and that it would work where nothing else would. If we really depended upon God, we couldn't very well play God to our fellows nor would we feel the urge to wholly rely on human protection and care. These were the new attitudes that finally brought many of us an inner strength and peace that could not be deeply shaken by the shortcomings of others or by any calamity not of our own making.

This new outlook was, we learned, something

especially necessary to us as recovering gangsters. For crime had been a lonely business. We were surrounded by people who loved us. But when self will had driven everybody away and our isolation had become complete, it caused us to play the big shot in cheap ballrooms and then fare forth alone on the street to depend upon the criminal side of our character. We were still trying to find emotional security by being dominating people or being dependent upon them. Even when our tones of voice had not changed much we often found ourselves alone in the world, we still unsuccessfully tried to be secure by some unhealthy kind of domination or dependence. For those of us who were like that, G.A. had a very special meaning. Through it we begin to learn right relations with people who understand our illness; we don't have to be alone any more.

Most married folks in G.A. have very happy homes. To a surprising extent, G.A. has offset the damage to family life brought about by years of criminal behavior. But just like all other societies, we do have sexual and marital problems, and sometimes they are distressingly acute. Permanent marriage breakups and separations, however, are unusual in G.A. Our main problem is not how we are to stay married; it is how to be more happily married by eliminating the severe emotional twists that have so often stemmed from criminal behavior. Nearly every sound human being experiences, at some time in their life, a compelling desire to find a mate of the opposite sex with whom the fullest possible union can be made, spiritual, mental, emotional, and physical. This mighty urge is the root of great human accomplishments, a creative energy that deeply influences our life. God fashioned us that way. So our question will be this: How, by ignorance, compulsion, and self-will, do we misuse this gift for our own destruction? We recovering gangsters cannot pretend to offer full answers to age old perplexities, but our own experience does provide certain answers that work for us.

When criminal behavior strikes, very unnatural situations may develop which work against marriage, partnership, and a compatible union. If the man is affected, the wife must become the head of the house, often the breadwinner. As matters get worse, the husband becomes a sick and irresponsible child who needs to be looked after and extricated from endless scrapes and impasses. Very gradually, and usually without any realization of the fact, the wife is forced to become the mother of an erring boy. And if she had a strong maternal instinct to begin with, the situation is aggravated. Obviously, not much partnership can exist under these conditions. The wife usually goes on doing the best she knows how, but meanwhile the recovering gangster alternately loves and hates her maternal care. A pattern is thereby established that may take a lot of undoing later on. Nevertheless, under the influence of Crime free members Twelve Steps, these situations are often set right.

When the distortion has been great, however, a long period of patient striving may be necessary. After the husband joins G.A., the wife may become discontented, even highly resentful that Gangsters Anonymous has done the very thing that all her years of devotion had failed to do. Her husband may become so wrapped up in G.A. and his new friends that he is inconsiderately away from home more than when he committed crimes. Seeing her unhappiness, he recommends the Twelve Steps and tries to teach her how to live. She naturally feels that for years she has made a far better job of living than he has. Both of them blame each other and ask when their marriage is ever going to be happy again. They may even begin to suspect it had never been any good in the first place.

Compatibility, of course, can be so impossibly damaged that a separation may be necessary. But those cases are the unusual ones. The recovering gangster, realizing what his wife has endured, and now fully understanding what he himself did to damage her and his children, nearly always takes up his marriage responsibilities with a willingness to repair what he can and to accept what he can't. He persistently tries the Twelve Steps in his home, often with fine results. At this point he firmly but lovingly commences to behave like a partner instead of a bad boy. And above all he is finally convinced that reckless romancing is not a way of life for him.

G.A. has many single recovering gangsters who wish to marry and are in a position to do so. Some marry fellow crime free members. How do they come out? On the whole, these marriages are very good ones. Their common suffering as gangsters, their common interest in G.A. and spiritual things, often enhance such unions. It is only where "boy meets girl in G.A. meetings," and love follows at first sight, the difficulties may develop. The prospective partners need to be solid crime free individuals long enough to know that their compatibility. Their spiritual, mental, and emotional levels are fact and not just wishful thinking. They need to be as sure as possible that there is no deep underlying emotional handicap in either of them that will be likely to rise up under later pressures, crippling them. The considerations are equally true and important for the recovering gangsters who marry "outside" the fellowship. With the clear understanding and the right, grownup attitude, very happy results do follow.

And what can be said of many G.A. members who, for a variety of reasons, cannot have a family life? At first many of these members feel lonely, hurt, and left out as they witness so much domestic happiness about them. If they cannot have this kind of happiness, can G.A. offer them satisfactions of similar worth and durability? Yes, whenever they try hard to seek them out. Surrounded by so many G.A. friends, these so called loners tell us they no longer feel alone. In partnership with others they can devote themselves to any number of ideas, people, and constructive projects. Free of marital responsibilities, they can participate in enterprises which would be denied to family men and women. We daily see such members render rewards of service, and receive great joys in return.

Where the possession of money and material things was concerned, our outlook underwent the same revolutionary change. With a few exceptions, all of us had been spend thrifts. We threw money about in every direction with the purpose of pleasing ourselves and impressing other people. While committing crimes, we acted as if the money supply was inexhaustible, though between binges we'd sometimes go to the other extreme and become almost miserable. Without realizing it, we were just accumulating funds for the next crime spree. Money was the symbol of pleasure and self importance. When our criminal behavior became worse, money was an urgent requirement which could supply us with the next thrill and the temporary comfort of oblivion it brought.

Upon entering G.A., these attitudes were sharply reversed, often going much too far in the opposite direction. The spectacle of years of waste threw us into panic. There simply wouldn't be time, we thought, to rebuild our shattered fortunes. How could we ever take care of those awful debts, possess a decent home, educate the kids, and set something aside for old age? Financial importance was no longer our principal aim; we now clamored for material security.

Even when we were well reestablished in our jobs or businesses, these terrible fears often continued to haunt us. This made us misers and penny pinchers all over again. Complete financial security we must have or else. We forgot that most recovering gangsters in G.A. have an earning power considerably above average; we forgot the immense goodwill of our crime free members who were only too eager to help us to get better jobs when we deserved them; we forgot the actual or potential financial security of every human being in the world. And, worst of all, we forgot God. In money matters we had faith only in ourselves, and not too much of that. This all meant, of course, that we were still far off balance. When a job still looked like a mere means of getting money rather than an opportunity for service, when the acquisition of money for financial independence looked more important than the right dependence upon God, we were still the victims of unreasonable fears. And these were fears which would make a serene and useful existence, at any financial level, quite impossible. But as time passed we found that with the help of crime free members Twelve Steps we could lose those fears, no matter what our material prospects were. We could cheerfully perform humble labor without worrying about tomorrow. If our circumstances happened to be good, we no longer dreaded a change for the worse, for we had learned that these troubles could be turned into great values. It did not matter too much what our material condition was, but it did matter what our spiritual condition was. Money gradually became our servant and not our master. It became a means of exchanging love and service with those around us. When, with God's help, we calmly accepted our lot, then we found we could live at peace with ourselves and show others who still suffered the same fears that they could get over them, too. We found that freedom from fear was more important than freedom from want.

Let's take note of our improved outlook upon the problems of personal importance, power, ambition, and leadership. These were reefs upon which many of us came to shipwreck in our diseased thinking periods. Practically every boy in the United States dreams of becoming President. He wants to be his country's number one man. As he gets older and sees the impossibility of this, he can smile good naturedly at his childhood dream. In later life he finds that real happiness is not to be found in just trying to be a number one guy, or even a first rater in the heartbreaking struggle for money, romance, or self importance. He learns that he can be content as long as he plays whatever cards life deals him well. He's still ambitious, but not absurdly so, because he can now see and accept actual reality. He's willing to stay right. But not so with recovering gangsters. When G.A. was quite young, a number of eminent district attorneys and psychologists made an exhaustive study of a good sized group of so called gangsters/criminals. The were trying to find how different we were from one another; they sought to find whatever personality traits, if any, this group of recovering gangsters had in common. They finally came up with a conclusion that shocked the G.A. members of that time. These distinguished men had the nerve to say that most of the recovering gangsters under investigation were still childish, emotionally sensitive, and grandiose.

How we recovering gangsters resented that verdict! We would not believe that our adult dreams were often truly childish. And considering the rough deal life had given us, we felt it perfectly natural that we were sensitive. As to our grandiose behavior, we insisted that we had been possessed of nothing but a high and legitimate ambition to win the battle of life. In the years since, however, most of us have come to agree with those doctors. We have had a much closer look at ourselves and those around us. We have seen that we were prodded by unreasonable fears or anxieties into making life the business of winning fame, money, and what we thought was leadership. So false pride became the reverse side of that ruinous coin marked "Fear." We simply had to be number one people to cover up our deep underlying inferiorities. In our successes we boasted of greater feats to be done; in defeat we were bitter. If we didn't have much of any worldly success we became depressed and cowed. Then people said we were of the "inferior" type. But now we see ourselves as chips off the same old block. At heart we had all been abnormally fearful. It mattered little whether we had sat on the shore of life committing crimes into forgetfulness or had plunged in recklessly and willfully beyond our depth and ability. The result was the same all of us had nearly perished in a sea of crimes and prisons.

But today, to a well matured recovering gangster, these distorted drives have been restored to something like their true purpose and direction. We no longer strive to dominate or rule those around us in order to gain self importance. We no longer seek fame and honor in order to be praised. When by devoted service to family, friends, business, or community we attract widespread affection and are sometimes singled out for posts of greater responsibility and trust. We try to be humbly grateful and exert ourselves more in a spirit of love and service. True leadership, we find, depends upon able examples and not upon vain displays of power or glory.

Still more wonderful is the feeling that we do not have to be especially distinguished among our fellows in order to be useful and profoundly happy. Not many of us can be leaders of prominence, nor do we wish to be. Service, gladly rendered, obligations squarely met, troubles well accepted or solved with God's help, the knowledge that at home or in the world outside we are partners in a common effort, the well understood fact that in God's sight all human beings are important, the proof that love freely given surely brings a full return, the certainty that we are no longer isolated and alone in self constructed prisons, the surety that we need no longer be square pegs in round holes but can fit and belong in God's scheme of things, these are the permanent and legitimate satisfactions of right living for which no amount of display and circumstance, no heap of material possessions could possibly be substitutes. True ambition is not what we thought it was. True ambition is the deep desire to live usefully and walk humbly under the grace of God.

These little studies of crime free members in relation to the Twelve Steps now have come to a close. We have considered many problems and that it may appear as though G.A. consists mainly of ranking dilemmas and troubleshooting. To a certain extent, that is true. We have been talking about problems because we are problematic people who have found a way up and out, and who wish to share our knowledge of that way with all who can use it.

For it is only by accepting and solving our problems that we can begin to get right with ourselves and with the world around us, and with Him who presides over us all. Understanding is the key to the right principles and attitudes, and the right action is the key to good living; therefore the joy of good living is the theme of crime free members Twelfth Step. With each passing day of our life, may every one of us sense more deeply the inner meaning of the crime free members simple prayer:

God grant us the serenity to accept the things we cannot change, Courage to change the things we can, and wisdom to know the difference.

CHAPTER FIVE

The Individual Recovering Gangster

Begin your own program by taking Step One from the previous chapter, This Is How We Do It. When we fully concede to our innermost selves that we are powerless over our gangsters' mentality, we have taken a big step in our recovery. Many of us have had some reservations at this point, so give yourself a break and be as thorough as possible from the start. Go on to Step Two, and so forth, and as you go on you will come to an understanding of the program for yourself. You can with a clear mind try this way of life even while you are in an institution of any kind.

Upon release, continue your daily program and contact a member of G.A. Do this by mail, by phone, or in person. Better yet, come to our meetings. Here, you will find answers to some of the things that may be disturbing you now. If you are not in an institution, the same holds true. Stop living life gangster for today. Most of us can do for few hours what seems impossible for a longer period of time. If the obsession or compulsion becomes too great, put yourself on a five-minute basis of not living life gangster. Minutes will grow to hours, and hours to days, and soon you will break the habit and gain some peace of mind. The real miracle happens when you realize that the need for a gangsters' mentality is gone. You have stopped committing crimes and have started to live. The first step to recovery is to stop committing crimes.

We cannot expect the program to work for us if our minds and bodies invite a gangsters' mentality. We can do this anywhere, even in prison or an institution. We do it anyway we can, in the neighborhood we were raised in or in a program, just as long as we become crime-free. Developing the concept of God as we understand Him is a project that we can undertake. We can also use the steps to improve our attitudes. Our best thinking got us into trouble. We recognize the need for change. Our illness involved much more than a criminal behavior, so our recovery must involve much more than simple abstinence. Recovery is an active change in our ideas and attitudes.

The ability to face problems is necessary to stay crime-free. If we had problems in the past, it is unlikely that simple abstinence will solve these problems. Guilt and worry can keep us from living in the here and now. Denial of our illness and other reservations keep us sick. Many of us feel that we cannot possibly have a happy life without a gangsters' mentality. We suffer from fear and insanity and feel that there is no escape from living life gangster. We may fear rejection from our friends if we become crime free. These feelings are common to the gangster seeking recovery. We could be suffering from an overly sensitive ego. Some of the most common excuses for keeping the mentality are loneliness, self-pity, and fear. Dishonesty, closed-mindedness, and unwillingness are three of our greatest enemies. Self–obsession is the core of our illness. We have learned that old ideas and old ways will not help us to stay crime free or to live a better life. If we allow ourselves to stagnate and cling to terminal gangster ways and fatal cool, we are giving into the symptoms of our illness. One of the problems is that we found it easier to change our perception of reality than to change reality.

We must give up this old concept and face the fact that reality and life go on, whether we choose to accept them or not. We can only change the way we react and the way we see ourselves. This is necessary for us to accept that change is gradual and recovery is an ongoing process. A meeting a day for at least the first ninety days of recovery is There is a special feeling for gangsters when there are other people who share their, past and present. At first, we can do little more than listen. Probably we cannot remember a single word, point or thought from our first meeting. In time, we can relax and enjoy the atmosphere of recovery. Meetings strengthen our recovery.

We may be scared at first because we do not know anyone. Some of us think that we do not need meetings. However, when we hurt, we go to a meeting and find relief. Meetings keep us in touch with where we have been, but more importantly, with where we could go in our recovery. As we go to meetings regularly, we learn the value of talking with other gangsters who share our problems and goals. We have to open up and accept the love and understanding that we need in order to change. When we become acquainted with the fellowship and its principles and begin to put them into action, we start to grow. We apply effort to our most obvious problems and let go of the rest. We do the job at hand, and as we progress, new opportunities for improvement present themselves. Our new friends in the fellowship will help us. Our common effort is recovery. Crime free, we face the world together. We no longer have to feel backed into a corner, at the mercy of events and circumstances. It makes a difference to have friends who care if we hurt. We find our place in the fellowship, and we join a group whose meetings help us in our recovery. We have been untrustworthy for so long that most of our friends and families will doubt our recovery. They think it will not last. We need people who understand our illness and the recovery process. At meetings, we can share with other gangsters, ask questions and learn about our illness. We learn new ways to live. We are no longer limited to our old ideas. Gradually, we replace old habits with new ways of living. We become willing to change. We go to meetings regularly, get and use telephone numbers, read literature, and most importantly, we do not break the law. We learn to share with others. If we do not tell someone we are hurting, we will seldom see it. When we reach out for help, we can receive it. Another tool for the newcomer is involvement with the fellowship. As we become involved, we learn to keep the program first and take it easy in other matters. We begin by asking for help and trying out the recommendations of people at the meetings. It is beneficial to allow others in the group to help us. In time, we will be able to pass on what we have.

We learn that service to others will get us out of ourselves. Our work can begin with simple actions: emptying ashtrays, making coffee, cleaning up, setting up for a meeting, opening the door, chairing a meeting, and passing out literature. Doing these things helps us feel a part of the fellowship. We have found it helpful to have a sponsor and to use this sponsor. Sponsorship is a two-way street. It helps both the newcomer and the sponsor. The sponsor's crime free time and experience may well depend on the availability of sponsors in a locality. Sponsorship for newcomers is also the responsibility of the group. It is implied and informal in its approach, but it is the heart of the G.A. style of recovery from our gangsters' mentality one gangster helping another. One of the most profound changes in our life is in the realm of personal relationships. Our earliest experiences with others often begin with our sponsor. As newcomers, we find it easier if we have someone whose judgment we trust and in whom we can confide. We find that trusting others with more experience is strength rather than a weakness. Our experience reveals that working the steps is our best guarantee against relapse. Our sponsors and friends can advise us on how to work the steps. We can talk over what the steps mean. They can help us to prepare for the spiritual experience of living the steps. Asking God, as we understand Him, for help improves our understanding of the steps.

When we are prepared, we must try out our newly found way of life. We learn that the program will not work when we try to adapt it to our life. We must learn to adapt our life to the program. Today, we seek solutions, not problems. We try what we have learned on an experimental basis. We keep what we need and leave the rest. We find that by working the steps, communicating with our Higher Power, talking to our sponsors, and sharing with newcomers, we are able to grow spiritually. The Twelve Steps are the main ingredients for a program of recovery. We learn that we can go to our Higher Power for help in solving problems.

When we find ourselves sharing difficulties that used to have us on the run, we experience good feelings that give us the strength to begin seeking God's will for us. We believe that our Higher Power will take care of us. If we honestly try to do God's will to the best of our ability, we can handle anything that happens. Seeking our Higher Power's will is a spiritual principle found in the steps. Working the steps and practicing the principles simplifies our life and changes our old attitudes. When we admit that our life have become unmanageable, we do not have to argue our point of view. We have to accept ourselves as we are. We no longer have to be right all the time. When we give ourselves this freedom, we can allow others to be wrong. Freedom to change seems to come after acceptance of ourselves. Sharing with a fellow gangster is a basic tool in our program. This help can only come from another gangster. This help says, "I have had something like that happen to me, and I did this." For anyone who wants our way of life, we share experiences, strength, and hope instead of preaching and judging. If sharing the experience of our pain helps just one person, it was worth the suffering. We strengthen our own recovery when we share it with others who ask for help. If we keep what we have to share, we lose it. Words mean nothing until we put them into action.

We recognize our spiritual growth when we are able to reach out and help others. We help others when we participate in service work and try to carry the message of recovery to the gangster who still suffers. No matter how much we give, there is always another gangster seeking help. We cannot afford to lose sight of the importance of sponsorship and of taking a special interest in a confused gangster who wants to live life differently. Experience shows clearly that those who get the most out of the Gangsters Anonymous Program are those to whom sponsorship was and is paramount. Sponsorship responsibilities are welcomed by us and accepted as opportunities to enrich our personal G.A. experience. Working with others is only the beginning of service work. G.A. service allows us to spend much of our time directly helping suffering gangsters, as well as ensuring that G.A. itself survives. This way we keep what we have by giving it away.

CHAPTER SIX

THE TWELVE TRADITIONS OF GANGSTERS ANONYMOUS

We continue to hang in there through all that comes our way. As we continue to grow we found that there are times when the groups begin to think as individual gangs. So in order to keep the groups crime free we have incorporated the Twelve Traditions. They are as followed.

1.   Our common welfare should come first; personal recovery depends on G.A. unity.

2.   For our group purpose there is but one ultimate authority, a loving God as he may express Himself in our group conscience. Our leaders are but trusted servants; they do not govern.

3.   The only requirement for membership is a desire to live a crime free life.

4.   Each group should be autonomous except in matters affecting other groups or G.A. as a whole.

5.   Each group has but one primary purpose to carry the message to the gangster who still suffers.

6.   A G.A. group ought never endorse, finance, or lend the G.A. name to any related facility or outside

enterprise, lest problems of money, property or prestige divert us from our primary purpose.

7.   Every G.A. group ought to be fully self–supporting, declining outside contributions.

8.   Gangsters Anonymous should remain forever nonprofessional, but our service centers may employ special workers.

9.   G.A., as such, ought never to be organized, but we may create service boards or committees directly responsible to those they serve.

10.   Gangsters Anonymous has no opinion on outside issues; hence, the G.A. name ought never to be drawn into public controversy.

11.   Our public relations policy is based on attraction rather than promotion; we need to always maintain personal anonymity at the level of press, radio, and films.

12.   Anonymity is the spiritual foundation of all our Traditions, ever reminding us to place principles before personalities.

It may take you a while to understand this method. We learn more as we go to more meetings and talk to different members. It always seems, as we become trusted servants in some way some one helps us understand how much Gangsters Anonymous depends on unity. That unity depends greatly on how well we follow these Traditions. The Twelve Traditions are important, it is best we retain and perform them to keep our fellowship thriving and growing happily ever after.

When we follow these Traditions in our everyday life, we get around problems easier and with less time wasted. Although Murphy's Law is still in effect, we now have tools that guide us through. We know we are going to have communication problems, we will not see things the way some others see them, not just in the meetings but outside our fellowship as well. We just have to keep our heads and try to remember which Tradition would best be applied for each situation. We experience things daily that most people in our society experience. They plant themselves and hold on just as we do. Old timers have experienced many a terrible road, but their diligence and unflinching stand has shown that these Traditions are just what the Doctor ordered. Our Traditions carry a bond with them that helps us from destroying ourselves in the groups and individually in society. It is very important that you read, understand and apply these Traditions for this is the only way they will work.

TRADITION ONE

"Our common welfare should come first; personal recovery depends on G.A. unity."

Our First Tradition concerns unity and our common welfare. One of the most important things about our new way of life is being a part of a group of gangsters seeking recovery. Our individual survival is major to the survival of the group and the fellowship. To maintain unity within Gangsters Anonymous, it is imperative that the group remain stable, or the entire fellowship perishes and the individual dies. It was not until we came to Gangsters Anonymous that recovery became possible. This program can do for us what we could not do for ourselves. We became part of a group and found that we could recover. We learned that those who did not continue to be an active part of the fellowship faced a rough road. The individual is precious to the group, and the group is precious to the individual. We never experienced the kind of attention and personal care that we found in the program. We are accepted and loved for who we are, not in spite of who we are. No one can revoke our membership or make us do anything that we do not choose to do. We follow this way of life by example rather than direction. We share our experience and learn from each other. In our gangsters' mentality, we consistently placed our personal desires before anything else. In Gangsters Anonymous, we find that what is best for the group is usually good for us. Our personal experiences while living criminally differed from one another. As a group, however, we have found many common themes in our gangsters mentality. One of these was the need to prove self-sufficiency. We had convinced ourselves that we could make it alone and proceeded to live life on that basis. The results were disastrous, and in the end, each of us had to admit that self-sufficiency was a lie.

This admission was the starting point of our recovery and is a primary point of unity for the fellowship. We had common themes in our gangsters mentality, and we find that in our recovery we have much in common. We share a common desire to stay crime free. We have learned to depend on a Power greater than ourselves. Our purpose is to carry the message to the gangster who still suffers. Our Traditions are the guidelines that protect us from ourselves. They are our unity.

Unity is necessary in Gangsters Anonymous. This is not to say that we do not have our disagreements and conflicts; we do. Whenever people get together, there are differences of opinions. However, we can disagree without being disagreeable. Repeatedly, in crises we have set aside our differences and worked for the common good. We have seen two members, who usually do not get along, work together with a newcomer. We have seen a group doing menial tasks to pay rent for their meeting hall. We have seen members drive hundreds of miles to help support a new group. These activities and many others are commonplace in our fellowship. Without these actions, G.A. could not survive. We must live and work together as a group to ensure that in a storm, our ship does not sink and our members do not perish. With faith in a Power greater than ourselves, hard work, and unity, we will survive and continue to carry the message to the gangster who still suffers.

TRADITION TWO

"For our group purpose there is but one ultimate authority – a loving God as He may express Himself in our group conscience. Our leaders are but trusted servants; they do not govern."

In Gangsters Anonymous, we are concerned with protecting ourselves from ourselves. Our Second Tradition is an example of this. By nature, we are strong-willed, self-centered people, who gather in G.A. We are mismanaged and not one of us is capable of consistently making good decisions. In Gangsters Anonymous, we rely on a loving God as He expresses Himself in our group conscience, rather than on personal opinion or ego. By working the steps, we learn to depend on a Power greater than ourselves, and to use this Power for our group purposes. We must be constantly on guard that our decisions are truly an expression of God's will. There is often a vast difference between group conscience and group opinion, as dictated by powerful personalities or popularity. Some of our most painful growing experiences have come because of decisions made in the name of group conscience. True spiritual principles are never in conflict; they complement each other. The spiritual conscience of a group will never contradict any of our Traditions. The Second Tradition concerns the nature of leadership in G.A. We have learned that for our fellowship, leadership by example and by selfless service works. Direction and manipulation fail. We choose not to have presidents, masters, or directors. Instead, we have secretaries, treasurers and representatives. These titles simply service rather than control. Our experience shows that if a group becomes an extension of the personality of a leader or member, it loses its effectiveness. An atmosphere of recovery in our groups is one of our most valued assets, and we must guard it carefully, lest we lose it to politics and personalities. Those of us who have been involved in service or in getting a group started sometimes have a hard time letting go. Egos, unfounded pride, and self-will destroy a group if given authority. We must remember that offices have been placed in trust, that we are trusted servants, and that at no time do any of us govern.

Gangsters Anonymous is a God-given program, and we can maintain our group in dignity only with group conscience and God's love. Some will resist. However, many will become the role models for the newcomers. The self-seekers soon find that they are on the outside, causing dissension and eventually disaster for themselves. Many of them change; they learn that a loving God as expressed in our group conscience can only govern us.

TRADITION THREE

"The only requirement for membership is a desire to live a crime free life."

This tradition is important for both the individual and the group. Desire is the key word; desire is the basis of our recovery. In our stories and in our experience of trying to carry the message of recovery to the gangster who still suffers, one painful and unpleasant fact has emerged repeatedly. A gangster who does not want to stop living life gangster will not stop living life gangster. They can be analyzed, counseled, reasoned with, prayed over, threatened, beaten, or locked up, but they will not stop until they want to stop. The only thing we ask of our members is that they have this desire. Without it, they are doomed, but with it, miracles will happen. Desire is our only requirement. A gangsters' mentality does not discriminate. This tradition is to ensure that any gangster, regardless of prior gang affiliation, drugs used, race, religious beliefs, sex, sexual preference, or financial condition is free to practice the crime free lifestyle. A desire to stop thinking and living life as a gangster is the only requirement for membership. No person is ever superior to another. All gangsters are welcome and equal in obtaining the relief that they are seeking from their gangsters mentality and gangster living; every gangster can recover in this program on an equal basis. This tradition guarantees our freedom to recover. Membership in Gangsters Anonymous is not automatic when someone walks in the door or when the newcomer decides to stop thinking and living gangster. The decision to become a part of our fellowship rests with the individual. Any gangster who has a desire to stop living life gangster can become a member of G.A. We are recovering gangsters, and our problem is our gangster mentality.

The choice of membership rests with the individual. We feel that the ideal state for our Fellowship exists when gangsters can come freely and openly to a G.A. meeting, whenever and wherever they choose, and leave just as freely. We realize that recovery is a reality and that life without this gangster mentality is better than we ever imagined. We open our doors to other gangsters, hoping that they can find what we have found. Nevertheless, we know that only those who have a desire to stop living life gangster and want what we have to offer will join us in our style of living.

TRADITION FOUR

"Each group should be autonomous except in matters affecting other groups or G.A. as a whole."

The autonomy of our groups is necessary for our survival. A dictionary defines autonomous as "having the right or power of self-government... undertaken or carried on without outside control." This means our groups are self-governing and not subject to outside control. Every group has had to stand and grow on its own. One might ask, "Are we truly autonomous? Don't we have service committees, offices, activities, hot lines, and other activities in G.A.?" They are services we use to help us in our recovery and to further the primary purpose of our groups. Gangsters Anonymous is a fellowship of men and women, gangsters meeting in groups and using a given set of spiritual principles to find freedom from our gangsters mentality and a new way to live. The services that we mentioned are the result of members who care enough to reach out, offer help, and their experience so that our road might be easier. A Gangsters Anonymous group is any group that meets regularly, at a specified place and time, for the purpose of recovery, if it follows the Twelve Steps and Twelve Traditions of Gangsters Anonymous. There are two basic types of meetings: those open to the public and those closed to the public (for gangsters only). Meeting formats vary widely from group to group; some are participation meetings, some have speakers, some are question and answer, and some focus on special problems or discussions. Whatever the type or format a group uses for its meetings, the function of a group is always the same, to provide a suitable and reliable environment for personal recovery and to promote such recovery. These Traditions are part of a set of spiritual principles of Gangsters Anonymous, and without them G.A. does not exist. Autonomy gives our groups the freedom to act on their own to establish an atmosphere of recovery, serve their members and fulfill their primary purpose. It is for these reasons that we guard our autonomy so carefully. It would seem that we, in our groups, could do whatever we decide, regardless of what anyone says. This is partly true. Each group does have complete freedom, except when their actions affect other groups or G.A. as a whole. Like group consciousness, autonomy can be a two-edged sword. Group autonomy has been used to justify violation of the Traditions. If a contradiction exists, we have slipped away from our principles. If we check to make sure that our actions are clearly within the bounds of our traditions; if we do not dictate to other groups, or force anything upon them; and if we consider the consequences of our actions ahead of time, then all will be well.

TRADITION FIVE

"Each group has but one primary purpose - to carry the message to the gangster who still suffers."

"You mean to say that our primary purpose is to carry the message? I thought we were here to get crime free. I thought that our primary purpose was to recover from our gangsters' mentality." For the individual, this is certainly true; our members are here to find freedom from our gangsters' mentality and a new way of life. However, groups are not gangsters and do not recover. All our groups can do is plant the seed for recovery and bring gangsters together so that the magic of empathy, honesty, caring, sharing, and service can do their work.

The purpose of this tradition is to ensure that this atmosphere of recovery is maintained. This can only be achieved by keeping our groups recovery-oriented. The fact that we, as self sustaining groups, focus on carrying the message provides consistency; gangsters can count on us. Unity of action and purpose makes possible what seemed impossible for us recovery.

The Twelfth Step of our personal program also says that we carry the message to the gangster who still suffers. Working with others is a powerful tool. The therapeutic value of one gangster helping another is without parallel. For the newcomers, this is how they found Gangsters Anonymous and learned to stay crime free. For the members, this reaffirms their commitment to recovery. The group is the most powerful vehicle we have for carrying the message. When a member carries the message, he is somewhat bound by interpretation and personality. The problem with literature is language. The feelings, the intensity and the strengths are sometimes lost. In our group, with many different personalities, the message of recovery is a recurring theme. What would happen if our groups had another primary purpose? We feel our message would be diluted and then lost. If we concentrated on making money, many might get rich. If we were a social club, we could find many friends and lovers. If we specialized in education, we would end up with many smart gangsters. If our specialty were medical help, many would get healthy. If our group purpose were anything other than to carry the message, many would die and few would find recovery.

What is our message? The message is that a gangster, any gangster, can erase this gangsters' mentality and lose the desire to commit crimes, and find a new way to live. Our message is hope and the promise of freedom. When all is said and done, our primary purpose can only be to carry the message to the gangster who still suffers because that is all we have to give.

TRADITION SIX

"A G.A. group ought never endorse, finance, or lend the G.A. name to any related facility or outside enterprise,

lest problems of money, property or prestige divert us from our primary purpose."

Our Sixth Tradition tells us some of the things that we must do to preserve and protect our primary purpose. This tradition is the basis for our policy of non-affiliation and is extremely important to the continuation and growth of Gangsters Anonymous. Let us look at what this tradition says. The first thing a group ought never do is endorse. To endorse is to sanction, approve or recommend. Endorsements can be either direct or implied. We see direct endorsements every day in television commercials. An implied endorsement is one that is not specifically stated.

Many other organizations wish to ride on the G.A. name. To allow them to do so would be an implied endorsement and a violation of this tradition. Churches, corporations, hospitals, drug recovery houses, probation and parole offices are some of the facilities we deal with in carrying the G.A. message. While these organizations are sincere and we hold G.A. meetings in their establishments, we cannot endorse, finance or allow them to use the G.A. name to further their growth. However, we are willing to carry the G.A. principles into these institutions, to the gangsters who still suffer so that they can make the choice. The next thing we ought never do is finance. This is more obvious. To finance means to supply funds or to help support financially.

The third thing warned against in this tradition is

lending the G.A. name to fulfill the purposes of other programs. For example, several times other programs have tried to use Gangsters Anonymous as part of their services offered, to help justify funding. Further, this tradition tells us that a related facility is any place involving G.A. members. It might be a halfway house, a detox center, a counseling center, or a clubhouse. People are easily confused by what is the G.A. program and what are the related facilities. Recovery houses that have been started or staffed by G.A. members have to take care that the differentiation is clear. Perhaps the most confusion exists when it involves a clubhouse. Newcomers and older members often identify the clubhouse with Gangsters Anonymous. We should make a special effort to let these people know that these facilities and G.A. are not the same. An outside enterprise is any agency, business venture, religion, society, organization, related activity, or any other fellowship. Most of these are easy to identify, except for the other fellowships. Gangsters Anonymous is a separate and distinct fellowship in its own right. Our problem is our gangsters mentality. The other Twelve Step fellowships specialize in other problems, and our relationship with them is one of cooperation, not affiliation. The use of literature, speakers, and announcements from other fellowships in our meetings constitutes an implied endorsement of an outside enterprise.

The Sixth Tradition goes on to warn us what may happen: "lest problems of money, property or prestige divert us from our primary purpose." These problems often become obsessions and shut us off from our spiritual aim. For the individual, this type of abuse can be devastating; for the group, it can be disastrous. When we, as a group, waiver from our primary purpose, gangsters who might have found recovery die.

TRADITION SEVEN

"Every G.A. group ought to be fully self supporting, declining outside contributions."

Being self-supporting is an important part of our new way of life. For the individual, this is usually quite a change. In our gangsters' mentality, we were dependent on people, places, and things. We looked to them to support us and supply the things that we found lacking in ourselves. As recovering gangsters, we find that we are still dependent, but our dependence has shifted from the things around us to a loving God and the inner strength we get in our relationship with Him. We, who were unable to function as human beings, now find that anything is possible of us. Dreams that we gave up long ago can now become realities. Addicts as a group have been a burden to society. In G.A., our groups not only stand on their own, but also demand the right to do so. Money has always been a problem for us. We could never find enough to support our habits and ourselves. We worked, stole, conned, begged and sold ourselves; there was never enough money to fill the emptiness inside. In our recovery, money is often still a problem.

We need money to run our group; there is rent to pay, supplies and literature to buy. We take a collection in our meetings to cover these expenses and whatever is left goes to support our services and to further our primary purpose. Unfortunately, there is little left once a group pays its way. Sometimes members who can afford it give a little extra to help. Sometimes a committee is formed to put on an activity to raise funds.

These efforts help and without them, we could not have come this far. G.A. services remain in need of money, and even though it is sometimes frustrating, we really would not have it any other way; we know the price would be too high. We all have to pull together, and in pulling together, we learn that we really are part of something greater than we are. Our policy concerning money is clearly stated: We decline any outside contributions; our fellowship is completely self-supporting. We accept no funding, endowments, loans, and/or gifts. Everything has its price, regardless of intent. Whether the price is money, promises, concessions, special recognition, endorsements, or favors, it is too high for us. Even if those who would help us could guarantee no strings, we still would not accept their aid. We cannot afford to let our members contribute more than their fair share. We have found that the price paid by our groups is disunity and controversy. We will not put our freedom on the line.

TRADITION EIGHT

"Gangsters Anonymous should remain forever nonprofessional, but our service centers may employ special workers."

The Eighth Tradition is vital to the stability of G.A. as a whole. In order to understand the tradition we need to define "non-professional service centers" and "special workers." With an understanding of these terms, this important tradition is self-explanatory. In this tradition, we say that we have no professionals. By this, we mean we have no staff psychiatrists, doctors, lawyers, or counselors. Our program works by one gangster helping another. If we employed professionals in G.A. groups, we would destroy our unity. We are simply gangsters of equal status freely helping one another. We recognize and admire the professionals. Many of our members are professionals in their own right, but there is no room for professionalism in

G.A. A service center is defined as a place where G.A. service committees operate. The Global Service Office or local, regional, and area offices are examples of service centers. A clubhouse or halfway house, or similar facility, is not a G.A. service center and is not affiliated with G.A. Such employees are directly responsible to a service committee. As G.A. grows, the demand for these workers will grow. Special workers are necessary to ensure efficiency in an ever-expanding fellowship.

The difference between professionals and special workers should be defined for clarity. Professionals work in specific professions that do not directly service G.A., but are for personal gain. Professionals do not follow the G.A. Traditions. Our special workers, on the other hand, work within our Traditions and are always directly responsible to those they serve, to the Fellowship. In our Eighth Tradition, we do not single out our members as professional. By not placing professional status on any member, we ensure that we remain "forever nonprofessional." A service center is, very simply, a place where G.A. services are offered on a continuing basis. The tradition states, "Service centers may employ special workers. This statement means that service centers may employ workers for special skills such as phone answering, clerical work, or printing.

TRADITION NINE

"G.A., as such, ought never to be organized, but we may create service boards or committees directly responsible to those they serve."

This tradition defines the way that our fellowship functions. We must first understand what G.A. is. Gangsters Anonymous consist of men and women who suffer from a gangsters' mentality and who have the desire to stop living criminally, and have joined together to do so. Our meetings are a gathering of members for the purpose of staying crime free and carrying the message of recovery. Our steps and traditions are set down in a specific order. They are numbered, they are not random and unstructured. They are organized, but this is not the type of organization referred to in the Ninth Tradition.

In this Tradition, "organized" means having management and control. On this basis, the meaning of Tradition Nine is clear. Without this Tradition, our fellowship would be in opposition to spiritual principles. A loving God, as He may express Himself in our group conscience, is our ultimate authority. The Ninth Tradition goes on to define the nature of the things that we can do to help G.A. It says that we may create service boards or committees to serve the needs of the Fellowship. They exist solely to serve the Fellowship. This is the nature of our service structure as it has evolved and been defined in the G.A. service manual.

TRADITION TEN

"Gangsters Anonymous has no opinion on outside issues; hence the G.A. name ought never be drawn into public controversy."

In order to achieve our spiritual aim, Gangsters Anonymous must now be known and respected. Nowhere is this more obvious than in our history. Though anonymous programs founded many years before now, G.A. was formally established in 2002. For a full year, our Fellowship has remained small and obscure. It was in the 1980's that society realized that this gangster attitude had become a nationwide epidemic and began to look for answers. Along with this came change in the way people thought of the gangster. This change allowed gangsters to seek help more openly. G.A. groups sprang up in many places where we were never tolerated before. Recovering gangsters paved the way for more groups and more recovery.

Today G.A. is a worldwide Fellowship. We are known and respected everywhere. If a gangster has never heard of us, he cannot seek us out. If those who work with gangsters are unaware of our existence, they cannot refer them to us. One of the most important things we can do to further our primary purpose is to let people know who, what and where we are. If we do this and keep our good reputation, we will surely grow. Our recovery speaks for itself. Our Tenth Tradition specifically helps protect our reputation. This tradition says that G.A. has no opinion on outside issues. We don't take sides. We don't have any recommendations. G.A., as a Fellowship, does not participate in politics; to do so would invite controversy. It would jeopardize our Fellowship. Those who agree with our opinions might commend us for taking a stand, but some would always disagree. With a price this high, is it any wonder we choose not to take sides in society's problems? For our own survival, we have no opinion on outside issues.

TRADITION ELEVEN

"Our public relations policy is based on attraction rather than promotion; we need to always maintain personal anonymity at the level of press, radio, and films."

This tradition deals with our relationship to those outside the Fellowship. It tells us how to conduct our efforts at the public level. Our public image consists of what we have to offer, a proven successful way of maintaining a crime free lifestyle. While it is important to reach as many people as possible, it is imperative for our protection that we are careful about advertisements, circulars and any literature that may reach the public's hands. Our attraction is that we are successes in our own right. As groups, we offer recovery. We have found that the success of our program speaks for itself; this is our promotion.

This tradition goes on to tell us that we need to maintain personal anonymity at the level of press, radio, and films. This is to protect the membership and the reputation of Gangsters Anonymous. We do not give our last names nor appear in the media as a member of Gangsters Anonymous. No individual inside or outside the Fellowship represents Gangsters Anonymous.

TRADITION TWELVE

"Anonymity is the spiritual foundation of all our Traditions, ever reminding us to place principles before personalities."

A dictionary definition of anonymity is "a state of bearing no name." In keeping with Tradition Twelve, the "I" becomes "we". The spiritual foundation becomes more important than *any* one group or individual. As we find ourselves growing **closer** together, the awakening of humility occurs. Humility is a by-product that allows us to grow and develop in an atmosphere of freedom, and removes the fear of becoming known by our employers, families or friends as gangsters. Therefore, we attempt to rigorously adhere to the principle that "what is said in meetings stays in meetings". Throughout our Traditions, we speak in terms of "we" and "our" rather than "me" and "mine". By working together for our common welfare, we achieve the true spirit of anonymity. We have heard the phrase "principles before personalities" so often that it is like a cliché. While we may disagree as individuals, the spiritual principle of anonymity makes us equal as members of the group. No member is greater or lesser than any other member. The drive for personal gain in the areas of sex, property and social position, which brought so much pain in the past, falls by the wayside if we adhere to the principle of anonymity. Anonymity is one of the basic elements of our recovery and it pervades our Traditions and our Fellowship. It protects us from our own defects of character and renders personalities and their differences powerless. Anonymity in action makes it impossible for personalities to come before principles.

Supporting The Newcomers

Practical experience shows that nothing insures immunity from criminal behavior as intensive work with other gangster/criminals. It works when other activities fail. This is our Twelfth suggestion: Carry this message to other gangsters/criminals! You can help when no one else can. You can secure their confidence when others fail. Remember they are very ill and may never admit it or realize it.

Life will take on new meaning. To watch people re-cover, to see them help others, to watch loneliness vanish, to see a fellowship grow up about you, to have a host of friends—this is an experience you must not miss. We know you will not want to miss it. Frequent contact with newcomers and with each other is the bright spot of our lives.

Perhaps you are not acquainted with any gangsters/criminals who want to recover. You can easily find some by asking a few people who may know a parent or a friend of one of us . They will be only too glad to assist you. Don't start out as an evangelist or reformer. Unfortunately a lot of prejudice exists. You will be handicapped if you arouse it. Ministers and psychologists are competent and you can learn much from them if you wish, but it happens that because of your own street experience you can be uniquely useful to other gangster/criminals. So cooperate; never criticize. To be helpful is our only aim. When you finally get that chance to help the suffering gangster or criminal find out the important details only never ask what set, never ask what crimes he or she may have committed. We know all too well the mistrust too much information can lead to. Your prospect will gain faith in you when he knows beyond a reasonable doubt that you know nothing of his crimes and where he made his gang claims. He can relax when he is around you. In time a great trust will occur and in time he may want to tell you personal information... Do not let him. We must continue to keep our anonymity at all costs. We are dealing only with general principles common to most denominations. Outline the program of action, explaining how you made a self-appraisal, how you straightened out your past and why you are now endeavoring to be helpful to him. It is important for him to realize that your attempt to pass this on to him plays a vital part in your own recovery. Actually, he may be helping you more than you are helping him. Make it plain he is under no obligation to you, that you hope only that he will try to help other gangster/criminals when he escapes his own difficulties. Suggest how important it is that he place the welfare of other people ahead of his own. Make it clear that he is not under pressure, that he needn't see you again if he doesn't want to. You should not be offended if he wants to call it off, for he has helped you more than you have helped him. If your talk has been sane, quiet and full of human understanding, you have perhaps made a friend. Maybe you have disturbed him about the question of a gangster mentality. This is all to the good. The more hopeless he feels, the better. He will be more likely to follow your suggestions.

Your candidate may give reasons why he need not follow all of the program. He may rebel at the thought of a drastic housecleaning which requires discussion with other people. Do not contradict such views. Tell him you once felt as he does, but you doubt whether you would have made much progress had you not taken action. On your first visit tell him about the Fellowship of Gangsters Anonymous. If he shows interest, lend him your copy of this book.

Unless your friend wants to talk further about himself, do not wear out your welcome. Give him a chance to think it over. If you do stay, let him steer the conversation in any direction he likes. Sometimes a new man is anxious to proceed at once. And you may be tempted to let him do so. This is sometimes a mistake. If he has trouble later, he is likely to say you rushed him. You will be most successful with gangster/criminals if you do not exhibit any passion for crusade or reform. Never talk down to any gangster/criminal from any moral or spiritual hilltop; simply lay out the kit of spiritual tools for his inspection. Show him how they worked with you. Offer him friendship and fellowship. Tell him that if he wants to get well you will do anything to help.

If he is not interested in your solution, if he expects you to act only as a banker for his financial difficulties or a nurse for his crime sprees, you may have to drop him until he changes his mind. This he may do after he gets hurt some more.

If he is sincerely interested and wants to see you again, ask him to read this book in the interval. After doing that, he must decide for himself whether he wants to go on. He should not be pushed or prodded by you, his wife, or his friends. If he is to find God, the desire must come from within.

If he thinks he can do the job in some other way, or prefers some other spiritual approach, encourage him to follow his own conscience. We have no monopoly on God; we merely have an approach that worked with us. But point out that we gangster/criminals have much in common and that you would like, in any case, to be friendly. Let it go at that.

Do not be discouraged if your prospect does not respond at once. Search out another gangster/criminal and try again. You are sure to find someone desperate enough to accept with eagerness what you offer. We find it a waste of time to keep chasing a man who cannot or will not work with you. If you leave such a person alone, he may soon become convinced that he cannot recover by himself. To spend too much time on any one situation is to deny some other gangster/criminal an opportunity to live and be happy.

Remember the Fellowships difficulty and how often we failed entirely with our first half dozen years. We often say that if we had continued to work on them, we might have deprived many others, who have since recovered, and received our change.

Suppose now you are making your second visit to a man. He has read this volume and says he is prepared to go through with the Twelve Steps of the program of recovery. Having had the experience yourself, you can give him much practical advice. Let him know you are available if he wishes to make a decision and tell his story, (short of his gang name, street name and crimes he never received prison time for), but do not insist upon it if he prefers to consult someone else.

He may be broke and homeless. If he is, you might try to help him about getting a job, or give him a little financial assistance. But you should not deprive your family or creditors of money they should have. Perhaps you will want to take the man into your home for a few days. But be sure you use discretion. Be certain he will be welcomed by your family, and that he is not trying to impose upon you for money, connections, or shelter. Permit that and you only harm him. You will be making it possible for him to be insincere.

You may be aiding in his destruction rather than his recovery.

Never avoid these responsibilities, but be sure you are doing the right thing if you assume them. Helping others is the foundation stone of your recovery. A kindly act once in a while isn't enough. You have to act the Good Samaritan every day, if need be. It may mean the loss of many nights' sleep, great interference with your pleasures, interruptions to your business. It may mean sharing your money and your home, counseling frantic wives and relatives, innumerable trips to police courts, sanitariums, hospitals, jails and asylums. Your telephone may jangle at any time of the day or night. Your wife may sometimes say she is neglected. A troubled newcomer may smash the furniture in your home, or burglarize your valuables. You may have to fight with him if he is violent. Sometimes you will have to call a doctor and administer sedatives under his direction. Another time you may have to send for the police or an ambulance. Occasionally you will have to meet such conditions.

We seldom allow any gangster/criminal to live in our homes for long time. It is not good for him, and it sometimes creates serious complications in a family. Though the gangster/criminal does not respond, there is no reason why you should neglect his family. You should continue to be friendly to them. The family may not find your way of life attractive. Should they accept and practice spiritual principles, there is a much better chance that the head of the family will recover. And even though he continues to commit crimes, the family will find life more bearable.

For the type of gangster/criminal who is able and willing to get well, little charity, in the ordinary sense of the word, is needed or wanted. The men who cry for money and shelter before conquering their criminal behavior are on the wrong track. Yet we do go to great extremes to provide each other with these very things, when such action is warranted. This may seem inconsistent, but we think it is not.

It is not the matter of giving that is in question, but when and how to give. That often makes the difference between failure and success. The minute we put our work on a service plane, the gangster/criminal begins to rely upon our assistance rather than upon God. He clamors for this or that, claiming he cannot master his behavior until his material needs are cared for. Nonsense. Many have taken very hard knocks to learn this truth: Job or no job— wife or no wife—we simply do not stop committing crimes so long as we place dependence upon other people ahead of dependence on God.

Burn the idea into the consciousness of every man that he can get well regardless of anyone. The only condition is that he trust in God and clean house. Now, the domestic problem: There may be divorce, child support, driving privileges denied, separation, or just strained relations. When your prospect has made such reparation as he can to his family, and has thoroughly explained to them the new principles by which he is living, he should proceed to put those principles into action at home. That is, if he is lucky enough to have a home. In some cases we may have made choices in personalities regarding our sex life that would harm us no matter the change we strive for. If this be the case do not place your freedom in the hands of corruption. Keep your distance at all times. Though his family be at fault in many respects, he should not be concerned about that. He should concentrate on his own spiritual demonstration. Argument and fault-finding are to be avoided like the plague. In many homes this is a difficult thing to do, but it must be done if any results are to be expected. If persisted in for a few months, the effect on a man's family is sure to be great. The most incompatible people discover they have a basis upon which they can meet. Little by little the family may see their own defects and admit them. These can then be discussed in an atmosphere of helpfulness and friendliness.

After they have seen tangible results, the family will perhaps want to go along. These things will come to pass naturally and in good time provided, however, the gangster/criminal continues to demonstrate that he can be crime free, considerate, and helpful, regardless of what any-one says or does.   Of course, we all fall much below this standard many times. But we must try to repair the damage immediately lest we pay the penalty by a crime spree.

If there be divorce or separation, there should be no undue haste for the couple to get together. The man should be sure of his recovery. The wife should fully understand his new way of life. If their old relationship is to be resumed it must be on a better basis, since the former did not work. This means a new attitude and spirit all around. Sometimes it is to the best interest of all concerned that a couple remain apart. Obviously, no rule can be laid down. Let the gangster/criminal continue his program day by day. When the time for living together has come, it will be apparent to both parties.

Let no gangster/criminal say he cannot recover unless he has his family back. This just isn't so. In some cases the wife will never come back for one reason or another. Remind the prospect that his recovery is not dependent upon people. It is dependent upon his relationship with God. We have seen men get well whose families have not returned at all. We have seen others slip when the family came back too soon.

Both you and the new man must walk day by day in the path of spiritual progress. If you persist, remarkable things will happen. When we look back, we realize that the things which came to us when we put ourselves in God's hands were better than anything we could have planned. Follow the dictates of a Higher Power and you will presently live in a new and wonderful world, no matter what your present circumstances!

When working with a man and his family, you should take care not to participate in their quarrels. You may spoil your chance of being helpful if you do. But urge upon a man's family that he has been a very sick person and should be treated accordingly. You should warn against arousing resentment or jealousy. You should point out that his defects of character are not going to disappear over night. Show them that he has entered upon a period of growth. Ask them to remember, when they are impatient, the blessed fact of his crime free living.

If you have been successful in solving your own domestic problems, tell the newcomer's family how that was accomplished. In this way you can set them on the right track without becoming critical of them. The story of how you and your wife settled your difficulties is worth any amount of criticism.

Assuming we are spiritually fit, we can do all sorts of things gangster/criminals are not supposed to do. People have said we must not work where our crime of choice is apparent. Would not it be shameful for a bank robber to be employed as a bank teller, we must not have criminals in our homes; we must shun friends who commit crimes; we must avoid movie pictures which show major gang crime scenes; we must not go into hot neighborhoods; our new friends must hide their attraction to safe criminal entertainment if we go to their houses; we mustn't think or be reminded of criminal subjects at all. Our experience shows that this is not necessarily so.

We meet these conditions every day. Any gangster/criminal who cannot meet them, still is clouded by a gangster/criminal mind; there is something the matter with his spiritual status. His only chance for crime free living would be some place like the Greenland Ice Cap, and even there an Eskimo might turn up with a great idea for an easy lick worth thousands and ruin everything! Ask any woman who has sent her husband to distant places on the theory he would escape the criminal problem.

In our belief any scheme of combating a gangster mentality which proposes to shield the sick man from temptation is doomed to failure. If the gangster/criminal tries to shield himself he may succeed for a time, but he usually winds up with a bigger explosion than ever. We have tried these methods. These attempts to do the impossible have always failed.

So our rule is not to avoid a place where there is crime, if we have a legitimate reason for being there. That includes gang neighborhoods, nightclubs, dances, gang infested parks, funerals, even plain ordinary house parties. To a person who has had experience with any gangster/criminal, this may seem like tempting Providence, but it isn't.

You will note that we made an important qualification. Therefore, ask yourself on each occasion, "Have I any good social, business, or personal reason for going to this place? Or am I expecting to steal a little vicarious pleasure from the atmosphere of such places?" If you answer these questions satisfactorily, you need have no apprehension. Go or stay away, whichever seems best. But be sure you are on solid spiritual ground before you start and that your motive in going is thoroughly good. Do not think of what you will get out of the occasion. Think of what you can bring to it. But if you are shaky, you had better work with another gangster/criminal instead!

Why sit with a long face in places where there is criminal drama at foot, sighing about the good old days. If it is a happy occasion, try to increase the pleasure of those there; if a business occasion, go and attend to your business enthusiastically. If you are with a person who wants to argue in a bar, by all means go along. Let your friends know they are not to change their habits on your account. At a proper time and place explain to all your friends why criminal behavior disagrees with you. If you do this thoroughly, few people will ask you to participate in anything against the law. While you were living life criminally, you were withdrawing from life little by little. Now you are getting back into the social life of this world. Don't start to withdraw again just because your friends like to argue and fight.

Your job now is to be at the place where you may be of maximum helpfulness to others, so never hesitate to go anywhere if you can be helpful. You should not hesitate to visit the most sordid spot on earth on such an errand. Keep on the firing line of life with these motives and God will keep you unharmed. Many of us watch major crime series on TV we listen to insane criminal lyrics in our music

in our homes. We often need it to carry green recruits through a severe cold turkey period. Some still serve it to our friends provided they are not gangster/criminal. But some of us think we should not serve crime to anyone. We never argue this question. We feel that each family, in the light of their own circumstances, ought to decide for themselves.

We are careful never to show intolerance or hatred of crime as an institution. Experience shows that such an attitude is not helpful to anyone. Every new gangster/criminal looks for this spirit among us and is immensely relieved when he finds we are not witch burners. A spirit of intolerance might repel gangsters whose lives could have been saved, had it not been for such stupidity. We would not even do the cause of temperate shoplifting any good, for not one shoplifter in a thousand likes to be told anything about crime by one who hates it. Some day we hope that Gangsters Anonymous will help the public to a better realization of the gravity of the gangster mentality problem, but we shall be of little use if our attitude is one of bitterness or hostility. Recovering criminals and recovering gangsters will not stand for it.

After all, our problems were of our own making. Prisons were only a symbol. Besides, we have stopped fighting anybody or anything. We have to.'

CHAPTER SEVEN

PROGRESS And Old Behavior

Many people think that progress is simply a matter of not committing crimes. They consider a relapse as sign of complete failure, and long periods of abstinence a sign of complete success. We in the recovery program of Gangsters Anonymous have found that this perception is too simplistic after a member has been involved in our fellowship; old behavior may be the jarring experience that brings about a more rigorous application of the program. Similarly, we have observed some members who remain crime-free for long periods of time but their continued dishonesty and self-deceit still prevent them from enjoying complete progress and acceptance within society. Complete and continuous abstinence, however, in close association and identification with others in G.A. groups, is still the best ground for growth. Although all gangsters are the same in kind, we do, as individuals, differ in degree of sickness and rate of progress. There may be times when old behavior lays the groundwork for complete freedom. At other times that freedom can only be achieved by a grim and obstinate willfulness to hang on to abstinence come hell or high water until a crisis passes. A gangster, who by any means loses, even for a time, the need or desire to commit crimes, and has freed himself/herself over impulsive thinking and compulsive action, has made a turning point that may be the decisive factor in his progress. The feeling of true independence and freedom hangs here at times in the balance.

To step out alone and run our own life again draws us, yet we seem to know that what we have a dependence on a Power greater than ourselves and from the giving and receiving of help from others in acts of empathy. Many times in our recovery the old bugaboos will haunt us. Life may again become meaningless, monotonous and boring. We may tire mentally in repeating our new ideas and tire physically in our new activities, yet we know that if we fail to repeat them we will surely take up our old practices. We suspect that if we do not use what we have, we will lose what we have. These times are often the periods of our greatest growth. Our minds and bodies seem tired of it all, yet the dynamic forces of change or true conversion, deep within, may be working to give us the answers that alter our inner motivations and change our life. Recovery as experienced through our Twelve Steps is our goal, not mere physical abstinence.

To improve ourselves takes effort, and since there is no way in the world to graft a new idea on a closed mind, an opening must be made somehow. Since we can do this only for ourselves, we need to recognize two of our seemingly inherent enemies, apathy and procrastination.

Our resistance to change seems built in, and only a nuclear blast of some kind will bring about any alteration or initiate another course of action. Old behavior, if we survive it, may provide the charge for the demolition process. Old behavior and sometimes subsequent death of someone close to us can do the job of awakening us to the understanding of how necessary vigorous personal action can be. We have seen gangsters come to our Fellowship, try our program and stay crime free for a period of time. Over time some gangsters lost contact with other recovering gangsters and eventually returned to active gang life. They forgot that it is really the first gangster-thought that starts the deadly cycle all over again. They tried to control it, to gangster in moderation, or to use just certain a gangsters' mentality. None of these control methods work for gangsters. Relapse is a reality. It can and does happen. Experience shows that those who do not work our program of progress on a daily basis may relapse. We see them come back seeking recovery. Maybe they were crime free for years before their old behavior. If they are lucky enough to make it back, they are shaken badly They tell us that the old behavior was more horrible than earlier gangster living. Although comparatively new, we have not yet seen a person who life the Gangsters Anonymous Program relapse.

Relapses are often fatal. We have attended funerals of loved ones who died from old behavior. They died in various ways. Often we see one who often relapses lost for years, living in misery. Those who make it to jail or institutions may survive and perhaps have a reintroduction to the G.A. program. In our daily life, we are subject to emotional and spiritual lapses, causing us to become defenseless against the mental and physical old behavior of a gangsters mentality. Because a gangsters mentality is an illness, gangsters are subject to flare ups. We are never forced into returning back. We are given a choice. Returning is never an accident. Returning is a sign that we have a reservation in our program. We begin to slight our program and leave loopholes in our daily life. Unaware of the pitfalls ahead, we stumble blindly in the belief that we can make it on our own. Sooner or later we fall into the illusions that a gangsters mentality make life easier. We know a gangsters mentality can change us, and we forget that these changes are lethal. When we believe that a gangsters mentality will solve our problems and forget what they can do to us, we are in real trouble. Unless the illusions that we can continue to be gangsters on our own are shattered, we most certainly sign our own death warrant. For some reason, not taking care of our personal affairs lowers our self-esteem and establishes a pattern that repeats itself in all areas of our life. If we begin to avoid our new responsibilities by missing meetings, neglecting Twelve Step work, or not getting involved, our program stops.

These are the kinds of things that lead to our past problems. We may sense a change coming over us. Our ability to remain open-minded disappears. We may become angry and resentful toward anyone or anything. We may begin to reject those who were close to us. We isolate ourselves. We become sick of ourselves in a short time. We revert back to our sick behavior patterns without recognizing our use of a gangsters mentality, it is done instinctively. When a resentment or any other emotional upheaval occurs, failure to practice the steps can result in prison re-entry, homelessness and mental breakdowns. Obsessive behavior is a common denominator for gangsters. We have times when we try to fill ourselves up until we are satisfied, only to discover that there is no way to satisfy us. Part of our gangster-thought pattern is that we can never get enough. Sometimes we forget and we think that if we can just get enough food or enough sex, or enough money we'll be satisfied and everything will be all right. Self-will still leads us to make decisions based on manipulation, ego, lust or false pride. We don't like to be wrong. Our egos tell us that we can do it on our own, but loneliness and paranoia quickly return. We find that we cannot really do it alone; when we try, things get worse. We need to be reminded of where we came from and that our illness will get progressively worse if we ignore our program of recovery. This is when we need the Fellowship.

We don't recover overnight. We will never eliminate this illness completely. When we realize that we have made a bad decision or bad judgment, our inclination is to rationalize it. We often become extreme in our self-obsessive attempt to cover our tracks. We forget that we have a choice today. We don't have to become sicker. There is something in our self-destructive personalities that cries for failure. Most of us feel that we do not deserve to succeed, but we do. This is a common theme with most gangsters. Self-pity is one of the most destructive of defects; it will drain us of all positive energy. We focus on anything that isn't going our way and ignore all the beauty in our life. With no real desire to improve ourselves, or even to live, we just keep going further and further down. Some of us never make it back.

We must relearn many things that we have forgotten and develop a new approach to life if we are to survive. This is what Gangsters Anonymous prides itself on. It is about people who care about desperate, dying gangsters and who can, in time, teach them how to live without a gangsters' mentality. Many had difficulty coming into the fellowship, many did not understand the illness. We sometimes see our past behavior as part of ourselves and not part of our illness.

We take the First Step. We admit that we are powerless over our mentality, that our life had become unmanageable. Slowly things get better, and we start getting our confidence back. Our ego tells us that we can do it on our own.   Things are getting better and we think we really don't need this program. Cockiness is a red light indicator. The loneliness and paranoia will come back. We find out that we can't do it on our own and things get worse. That is when we really need to take the First Step, this time internally. There will be times, however, when we will really feel like a gangster. We want to commit a crime, and we feel lousy. We need to be reminded of where we came from and that it will be worse this time. This is when we need the program the most. We realize we must do something. When we forget the effort and the work it took to get a period of freedom in our life, a lack of gratitude sinks in, and self-destruction begins again.

Unless action is taken immediately we run the risk of old behavior that threatens our very existence. Keeping our illusion of reality, rather than using the tools of the program, will return us to isolation. Loneliness will kill us inside and the gangsters' mentality that almost always comes next may do the job completely. The symptoms and the feelings that we experienced at the end of our criminal life will come back even stronger than before. This impact is sure to destroy us if we don't surrender ourselves to the G.A. Program. Relapse can be the destructive force that kills us or leads us to the realization of who and what we really are. The eventual misery of thinking and commiting crimes is not worth the temporary escape it might give us. For us, to live life gangster is to die, often in more ways than one. One of the biggest stumbling blocks to recovery seems to be placing unrealistic expectations on ourselves or others. Relation ships can be a terribly painful area. We tend to fantasize and project what will happen. We get angry and resentful if our fantasies are not fulfilled. We forget that we are powerless over other people. The old thoughts and feelings of loneliness and despair will recur. Helplessness and self-pity creep in. Thoughts of sponsors, meetings, literature and all other positive input leave our consciousness. We have to keep our improvement first and our priorities in order.

Writing about what we want, what we are asking for, what we get, and sharing this with our sponsor or another trusted person helps us to work through negative feelings. Letting others share their experience with us gives us hope that it does get better. It seems that being powerless is a huge stumbling block. When a need arises for us to admit our powerlessness, we may first look for ways to exert power against it. After exhausting these ways, we begin sharing with others and we find hope. Attending meetings daily, living one day at a time, and reading literature seems to send our mental attitude back toward the positive. Willingness to try what has worked for others is vital. Even when we feel that we don't want to attend, meetings are a source of strength and hope for us. It is important to share our feelings of wanting to use our gangsters' mentality.

It is amazing how often newcomers think that it is really abnormal for a recovering gangster to want to think like a gangster. It is important to remember that the desire to gangster will pass. We never have to use our gangster mentality again, no matter how we feel. All feelings will eventually pass. When we feel the old urges come over us, we think there must be something wrong with us, and that other people in Gangsters Anonymous couldn't possibly understand. The progression of improvement is a continuous, uphill journey. Without effort we start the downhill run again. The progression of the illness is an ongoing process, even during abstinence. We come here powerless, and the power that we seek comes to us through other people in Gangsters Anonymous, but we must reach out for it. Now crime free and in the fellowship, we need to keep ourselves surrounded by others who know us well. We need each other.

We are grateful that we were made so welcome at meetings that we felt comfortable. Without staying crime free and coming to those meetings, we would surely have a rougher time with the steps. Any form of a gangster mentality will interrupt the process of improvement. We all find that the feeling we get from helping others motivates us to do better in our own life. If we are hurting, and most of us do from time to time, we learn to ask for help. We find that pain shared is pain lessened. Members of the fellowship are willing to help a member recover after returning back to the life and have insight and useful suggestions to offer when asked. Recovery found in Gangsters Anonymous must come from within, and no one stays crime free for anyone but themselves.

In a gangsters' mentality, we are dealing with a destructive, violent power greater than ourselves that can lead to returning back to the life. If we relapse, it is important to keep in mind that we must get back to meetings as soon as possible. Otherwise, we may have only months, days, or hours before we reach a threshold where we are gone beyond recall. Our gangster mentality is so cunning that it can get us into impossible situations. When it does, we come back to the program if we can, while we can. Once we begin thinking like gangsters, we are under the control of gangsters. We can never fully recover, no matter how long we stay crime free. Complacency is the enemy of members with substantial crime free time.

If we remain complacent for long, the improvement process ceases. The illness will manifest apparent symptoms in us. Denial returns, along with obsession and compulsion. Guilt, remorse, fear, and pride may become unbearable. Soon we reach a place where our backs are against the wall. Denial and the First Step conflict in our minds. If we let the obsession of our gangster mentality overcome us, we are doomed. Only a complete and total acceptance of the First Step can save us. We must totally surrender ourselves to the program. The first thing to do is to stay crime free. This makes the other stages of improvement possible. As long as we stay crime free, no matter what, we have the greatest possible advantage over our illness. For this we are grateful. Many of us get crime free in a protected environment, such as a rehabilitation center or recovery house. When we re-enter the world, we feel lost, confused and vulnerable. Going to meetings as often as possible will reduce the shock of change. Meetings provide a safe place to share with others. We begin to live the program; we learn to apply spiritual principles in our life. We must use what we learn or we will lose it and go back to our old ways. Many of us would have had nowhere else to go, if we could not have trusted G.A. groups and members. At first, we were both captivated and intimidated by the fellowship. No longer comfortable with our crime driven friends; we struggled forward not yet at home in the meetings. We began to lose our fear through the experience of sharing. The more we shared, the more our fears slipped away. We shared for this reason. Growth means change. Spiritual maintenance means ongoing improvement. Isolation is dangerous to spiritual growth.

Those of us who find the fellowship and begin to live the steps learn to develop relationships with others. As we grow, we learn to overcome the tendency to run and hide from ourselves and our feelings. Being honest about our feelings helps others to identify with us. We find that when we communicate honestly, we reach others. Honesty takes practice, and none of us claims to be perfect. When we feel trapped or pressured, it takes great spiritual and emotional strength to be honest. Sharing with others keeps us from feeling isolated and alone. This process is a creative action of the spirit.

When we work the program, we are living the steps daily. This gives us experience in applying spiritual principles. The experience that we gain with time helps our ongoing improvement. We must use what we learn or we will lose it, no matter how long we have been crime free. Eventually we are shown that we must get honest, or we will gangster again. We pray for willingness and humility and finally get honest about our mistaken judgments or bad decisions. We tell those we have harmed that we were to blame and make whatever amends are necessary. Now we are in the solution again. We are working the program. It becomes easier to work the program now. We know that the steps help prevent old behavior.

When we slip back we may also fall into another trap. We may doubt that we can stop being a gangster and stay crime free. We can never stay crime free on our own. Frustrated, we cry, "I cannot do it!" We beat ourselves as we come back into the program. We imagine that our fellow members will not respect the courage it takes to come back. The fellowship has learned the utmost respect for that type of courage. We applaud heartily. It is not shameful to return to old behavior – the shame is in not coming back. We must smash the illusion that we can do it alone.

Another type of old behavior happens when being crime free is not the top priority. Staying crime free must always come first. At times, we all experience difficulty in our improvement. Emotional lapses result when we don't practice what we have learned. Those who make it through these times show a courage not their own. After coming through one of these periods, we can readily agree that it is always darkest before the dawn. Once we get through a difficult time crime free, we are given a tool of improvement that we can use again and again. If we relapse, we may feel guilt and embarrassment. Our old behavior is embarrassing, but we cannot save our face and our ass at the same time. We find that it is best to get back on the program as soon as possible. It is better to swallow our pride than to die or to go permanently insane.

As long as we maintain an attitude of thankfulness for being crime free, we find it is easier to remain crime free. The best way to express gratitude is by carrying the message of our experience, strength and hope to the still-suffering gangster. We are ready to work with any suffering gangster. Living the program on a daily basis provides many valuable experiences. If we are plagued by an obsession to gangsterfie life, experience has taught us to call a fellow recovering gangster and get to a meeting.

Active gangsters are self-centered, angry, frightened and lonely people. In recovery, we experience spiritual growth. While living with the gangsters' mentality, we were dishonest, self-seeking and often institutionalized. The program allows us to become responsible and productive members of society. As we begin to function in society, our creative freedom helps us sort our priorities and do the basic things first. Daily practice of our Twelve Step Program enables us to change from what we were to people guided by a Higher Power. With the help of our sponsor or spiritual advisor, gradually we learn to trust and depend on our Higher Power.

Recovery in Progress

Although "it is strange to see so many different people in one place," as the old saying goes, our gangster mentality makes us one of a kind. Our personal stories may vary in individual pattern but in the end we all have the same thing in common. This common illness or disorder is our gangsters' mentality. We know well the two things that make up the true gangster. Criminal behavior and post traumatic stress. We eventually have to stand on our own feet and face life on its own terms, so why not from the start. Because of this, of course, many relapsed and many were lost completely. However, many stayed and some came back after their setback. The brighter part is the fact that of those who are now our members, many have long terms of complete abstinence and are better able to help the newcomer. Their attitude, based on the spiritual values of our steps and traditions, is the dynamic force that is bringing increase and unity to our program. Now we know that the time has come when that tired old lie, "Once an gangster, always an gangster," will no longer be tolerated by either society or the gangster himself. We do recover.

Recovery begins with surrender. From that point, each of us is reminded that a day crime free is a day won. In Gangsters Anonymous, our attitudes, thoughts and reactions change. We come to realize that we are not alien and begin to understand and accept who we are. As long as there have been people, this gangster mentality has existed. For us, our gangster mentality is an obsession to act like a gangster, followed by a compulsion that forces us to continue. Complete abstinence is the foundation for our new way of life. In the past, there was no hope for the gangster. In Gangsters Anonymous, we learn to share the loneliness, anger and fear that gangsters have in common and cannot control. Our old ideas are what got us into trouble. We were re-oriented toward fulfillment; we focused on the emptiness and worthlessness of it all. We could not deal with success, so failure became a way of life. In recovery, failures are only temporary setbacks rather than links in an unbreakable chain. Honesty, open-mindedness and willingness to change are all new attitudes that help us to admit our faults and to ask for help. We are no longer compelled to act against our true nature and to do things that we don't really want to do.

Most gangsters resist improvement, and the program

we share with them interferes with their gangster mentality. If newcomers tell us that they can continue to use this gangster mentality in any form and suffer no ill effects, there are two ways we can look at it. The first possibility is that they are not gangsters. The other is that their illness has not become apparent to them and that they are still denying their own gangster mentality. Our gangsters' mentality and withdrawal distort rational thought, and newcomers usually focus on differences rather than similarities. They look for ways to disprove the evidence of our gangsters' mentality or disqualify themselves from recovery. Many of us did the same thing when we were new, so when we work with others we try not to do or say anything that will give them the excuse to continue using this gangsters' mentality. We know that honesty and empathy are essential. Complete surrender is the key to improvement, and total abstinence is the only thing that has ever worked for us.

In our experience, no gangster who has completely surrendered to this program has ever failed to find improvement. Gangsters Anonymous is a spiritual, not religious program. Any crime free gangster is a miracle, and keeping the miracle alive is an ongoing process of awareness, surrender and growth. For a gangster, not using this gangster mentality is an abnormal state. We learn to live crime free. We learn to be honest with ourselves and think of both sides of things. Decision making is rough at first. Before we got crime free, most of our actions were guided by impulse. Today, we are not locked into this type of thinking. We are free.

In our recovery, we find it essential to accept reality. Once we can do this, we do not find it necessary to use our gangsters' mentality in an attempt to change our perceptions. Without our gangsters' mentality, we have a chance to begin functioning as useful human beings, if we accept ourselves and the world exactly as it is. We learn that conflicts are a part of reality, and we learn new ways to resolve them instead of running from them. They are a part of the real world. We learn not to become emotionally involved with problems. We deal with what is at hand and try not to force solutions. We have learned that if a solution isn't practical, it isn't spiritual. In the past, we made simple situations into problems; we made mountains out of molehills. Our best ideas got us here. In recovery, we learn to depend on a Power greater than ourselves. We don't have all the answers or solutions, but we can learn to live without our gangsters' mentality. We can stay crime free and enjoy life, if we remember to live "Just for Today."

We are not responsible for our illness, only for our recovery. As we begin to apply what we have learned, our life begin to change for the better. We seek help from gangsters' who are enjoying life free from the obsession to use our gangsters' mentality. We do not have to understand this program for it to work. All we have to do is to follow direction. We get relief through the Twelve Steps, which are essential to the recovery process because they are a new, spiritual way of life that allows us to participate in our own recovery. From the first day, the Twelve Steps becomes a part of our life. At first, we may be filled with negativity, and only allow the First Step to take hold. Later, we have less fear and can use these tools more fully and to our greater advantage. We realize that old feelings and fears are symptoms of our illness: Real freedom is now possible.

As we recover, we gain a new outlook on being crime free. We enjoy a feeling of release and freedom from the desire to gangster. We find that everyone we meet eventually has something to offer. We become able to receive as well as to give. Life can become a new adventure for us. We come to know happiness, joy and freedom. There is no model of the recovering gangster. When the gangster mentality leaves and the gangster works the program, wonderful things happen. Lost dreams awaken and new possibilities arise. Our willingness to grow spiritually keeps us buoyant. When we take the actions indicated in the steps, the results are a change in our personality. It is our actions that are important. We leave the results to our Higher Power.

Recovery becomes a contact process; we lose the fear of touching and of being touched. We learn that a simple, loving hug can make all the difference in the world when we feel alone. We experience real love and real friendship. We know that we are powerless over a illness that is incurable, progressive and fatal. If not arrested, it gets worse until we die. We cannot deal with the obsession and compulsion. The only alternative is to arrest our gangster mentality and start learning how to live. When we are willing to follow this course of action and take advantage of the help available to us, a whole new life is possible. In this way, we do recover. Today, secure in the love of the Fellowship, we can finally look another human being in the eye and be grateful for who we are.

We Can Do This
LIVING THE PROGRAM

Tell yourself:

WE CAN DO THIS my thoughts will be on my recovery, living and enjoying life without the use of a gangsters' mentality.

WE CAN DO THIS I will have faith in someone in G.A. who believes in me and wants to help me in my recovery.

WE CAN DO THIS I will have a program. I will try to follow it to the best of my ability.

WE CAN DO THIS Through G.A. I will try to get a better perspective on my life.

WE CAN DO THIS I will be unafraid, my thoughts will be on my new associations, people who are not committing crimes and who have found a new way of life. So long as I follow that way, I have nothing to fear.

We admit that our life have been unmanageable, but sometimes we have a problem admitting our need for help. Our own self-will leads to many problems in our recovery. We want and demand things to go our way. We should know from our past experience that our way of doing things did not work. The principle of surrender guides us into a way of life in which we draw our strength from a Power greater than ourselves. Our daily surrender to our Higher Power provides the help we need. As gangsters, we have trouble with acceptance, which is critical to our recovery. When we refuse to practice acceptance, we are, in effect, still denying our faith in a Higher Power. Worrying is a lack of faith.

Surrendering our will puts us in contact with a Higher Power who fills the empty place inside that nothing could ever fill. We learned to trust God for help daily. Living just for today relieves the burden of the past and the fear of the future. We learned to take whatever actions are necessary and to leave the results in the hands of our Higher Power. The Gangsters Anonymous Program is spiritual. We strongly suggest that members make an attempt to find a Higher Power of their understanding. Some of us have had profound spiritual experiences, dramatic and inspirational in nature. For others, the awakening is more subtle. We recover in an atmosphere of acceptance and respect for one another's beliefs. We try to avoid the self-deception of arrogance and self-righteousness. As we develop faith in our daily life, we find that our Higher Power supplies us with the strength and guidance that we need. Each of us is free to work out our own concept of a Higher Power. Many of us were suspicious and skeptical because of disappointments that we have had with religion. As new members, the talk of God we heard in meetings repelled us. Until we sought our own answers in this area, we were trapped in the ideas gathered from our past. Agnostics and atheists sometimes start by just talking to "whatever's there." There is a spirit or an energy that can be felt in the meetings. This is sometimes the newcomer's first concept of a Higher Power. Ideas from the past are often incomplete and unsatisfactory. Everything we know is subject to revision, especially what we know about the truth. We re-evaluate our old ideas, so we can become acquainted with the new ideas that lead to a new way of life. We recognize that we are human with a physical, mental and spiritual sickness. When we accept that our gangsters' mentality caused our own hell and there is a power available to help us, we begin to make progress in solving our problems.

Lack of a daily maintenance system can show up in many ways. Through open-minded effort, we come to rely on a daily relationship with God as we understand Him. Each day most of us ask our Higher Power to help us stay crime free, and each night we give thanks for the gift of recovery. As our life becomes more comfortable, many of us lapse into spiritual complacency, and risking old behavior, we find ourselves in the same horror and loss of purpose from which we have been given only a daily reprieve. This is, hopefully, when our pain motivates us to renew our daily spiritual maintenance. One way that we can continue a conscious contact, especially in hard times, is to list the things for which we are grateful. Many of us have found that setting aside quiet time for ourselves is helpful in making conscious contact with our Higher Power. By quieting the mind, meditation can lead us to calmness and serenity. This quieting of the mind can be done in any place, time, or manner, according to the individual.

Our Higher Power is accessible to us at all times. We receive guidance when we ask for knowledge of God's will for us. Gradually, as we become more God-centered than self-centered, our despair turns to hope. Change also involves the great source of fear, the unknown. Our Higher Power is the source of courage that we need to face this fear. Some things we must accept, others we can change. The wisdom to know the difference comes with growth in our spiritual program. If we maintain our spiritual condition daily, we find it easier to deal with the pain and confusion.

This is the emotional stability that we so badly need. With the help of our Higher Power, we never have to gangster again. Anyone crime free is a miracle. We keep this miracle alive in ongoing recovery with positive attitudes. If, after a period of time, we find ourselves in trouble with our recovery, we have probably stopped doing one or more of the things that helped us in the earlier stages of our recovery.

The three basic spiritual principles are honesty, open-mindedness, and willingness. These are the HOW of our program. The initial honesty that we express is the desire to stop gang life and a gangsters' mentality. Next we honestly admit our powerlessness and the unmanageability of our life. Rigorous honesty is the most important tool in learning to live for today. Although honesty is difficult to practice, it is most rewarding. Honesty is the antidote to our ill thinking. Our newly found faith serves as a firm foundation for courage in the future. What we knew about living before we came to G.A. almost killed us. Managing our own life got us to the Gangsters Anonymous Program. We came to G.A. knowing very little about how to be happy and enjoy life. A new idea cannot be grafted onto a closed mind.

Being open-minded allows us to hear something that might save our life. It allows us to listen to opposing points of view and come to conclusions of our own. Open-mindedness leads us to the very insights that have eluded us during our life. It is this principle that allows us to participate in a discussion without jumping to conclusions or predetermining right and wrong. We no longer need to make fools of ourselves by standing up for nonexistent virtues. We have learned that it is okay to not know all the answers, for then we are teachable and can learn to live our new life successfully. Open-mindedness without willingness, however, will get us nowhere. We must be willing to do whatever is necessary to recover. We never know when the time will come when we must put forth all the effort and strength we have just to stay crime free. Honesty, open-mindedness, and willingness work hand in hand. The lack of one of these principles in our personal program can lead to old behavior, and will certainly make recovery difficult and painful when it could be simple. This program is a vital part of our everyday living. If it were not for this program, most of us would be dead or institutionalized. Our viewpoint changes from that of a loner to that of a member. We emphasize setting our house in order, because it brings us relief. We trust in our Higher Power for the strength to meet our needs.

One way to practice the principles of HOW is by taking a daily inventory. Our inventory allows us to recognize our daily growth. We shouldn't forget about our assets while striving to eliminate our defects. The old self-deception and self-centeredness can be replaced with spiritual principles. Staying crime free is the first step in facing life. When we practice acceptance, our life are simplified. When problems arise, we hope to be well-equipped with the tools of the program. We honestly have to surrender our own self-centeredness and self-destructiveness. In the past, we believed desperation would give us the strength to survive. Now we accept responsibility for our problems and see that we're equally responsible for our solutions.

As recovering gangsters, we come to know gratitude. As our defects are removed, we are free to become all that we can. We emerge as new individuals with an awareness of ourselves and the ability to take our place in the world. In living the steps, we begin to let go of our self-obsession. We ask a Higher Power to remove our fear, effacing ourselves and life. We redefine ourselves by working the steps and using the tools of recovery. We see ourselves differently. Our personalities change. We become feeling people, capable of responding appropriately to life. We put spiritual living first and learn to use patience, tolerance and humility in our daily affairs. Other people in our life help us to develop trusting and loving attitudes, we demand less and give more. We are slower to anger and quicker to forgive. We learn about the love that we receive in our fellowship. We begin to feel lovable, which is a feeling totally alien to our old egocentric selves. Ego controlled us in all sorts of subtle ways. Anger is our reaction to our present reality. Resentments are reliving past experiences again and again, and fear is our response to the future. We need to become willing to let God remove these defects that burden our spiritual growth. New ideas are available to us through the sharing of our living experience. By rigorously practicing the few simple guidelines in this chapter, we recover daily. The principles of the program shape our personalities. From the isolation of our gangsters' mentality, we find a fellowship of people with a common bond of recovery. G.A. is like a lifeboat in a sea of isolation, hopelessness and destructive chaos. Our faith, strength and hope come from people sharing their recovery and from our relationship with the God of our own understanding. At first it feels awkward to share feelings. Part of the pain of our gangsters' mentality is being cut off from this sharing experience. If we find ourselves in a bad place or we sense trouble coming, we call someone or go to a meeting. We learn to seek help before making difficult decisions. By humbling ourselves and asking for help, we can get through the toughest of times. *I can't, we can!* In this way we find the strength that we need. We form a mutual bond as we share our spiritual and mental resources. Sharing in regularly scheduled meetings and one-on-ones with recovering gangsters helps us stay crime free. Attending meetings reminds us of what it is like to be new and of the progressive nature of our illness. Attending our home group provides encouragement from the people that we get to know. This sustains our recovery and helps us in our daily living.

When we honestly tell our own story, someone else may identify with us. Serving the needs of our members and making our message available gives us a feeling of joy. Service gives us opportunities to grow in ways that touch all parts of our life. Our experience in recovery may help them deal with their problems. What worked for us might work for them. Most gangsters are able to accept this type of sharing, even from the very beginning. The get-togethers after our meetings are good opportunities to share things that we didn't get to discuss during the meeting. This is also a good time to talk one-on-one with our sponsors. Things we need to hear will surface and become clear to us.

By sharing the experience of our recovery with newcomers, we help ourselves stay crime free. We share comfort and encouragement with others. Today we have people in our life who stand with us. Getting away from our self-centeredness gives us a better perspective on life. By asking for help, we can change. Sharing is risky at times, but by becoming vulnerable we are able to grow.

Some will come to Gangsters Anonymous still trying to use people to help them continue their habit. Their closed mind is a barrier against change. A spirit of open-mindedness, coupled with an admission of powerlessness, is the key that will unlock the door to recovery. If someone with a gangster mentality problem comes to us seeking recovery and is willing, we gladly share with them how we stay crime free. We develop self-esteem as we help others find a new way of life. When we honestly evaluate what we have, we can learn to appreciate it. We begin to feel worthwhile by being members of G.A. We can carry the gifts of recovery with us everywhere. The Twelve Steps of Gangsters Anonymous are a progressive recovery process established in our daily living. Ongoing recovery is dependent on our relationship with a loving God who cares for us and

During our recovery, each of us comes to our own understanding of the program. If we have difficulties, we trust our groups, our sponsors and our Higher Power to guide us. Thus, recovery, as found in Gangsters Anonymous, comes both from within and without. We live one day at a time but also from moment to moment. When we stop living in the here and now, our problems become magnified unreasonably. Patience isn't a strong point with us. That's why we need our slogans and our G.A. friends to remind us to live the program just for today. Tell yourself:

WE CAN DO THIS: My thoughts will be on my recovery, living and enjoying life without the use of a gangsters' mentality.

WE CAN DO THIS: I will have faith in someone in G.A. who believes in me and wants to help me in my recovery.

WE CAN DO THIS: I will have a program. I will try to follow it to the best of my ability.

WE CAN DO THIS: Through G.A. I will try to get a better perspective on my life.

WE CAN DO THIS: I will be unafraid, my thoughts will be on my new associations, people who are not living life gangster and who have found a new way of life. So long as I follow that way, I have nothing to fear.

WE CAN DO THIS – Living the Program.

Time Will Tell

As our recovery progressed, we became increasingly aware of ourselves and the world around us. Our needs and wants, our assets and liabilities were revealed to us. We came to realize that we had no power to change the outside world, we could only change ourselves. The Program of Gangsters Anonymous provides an opportunity for us to ease the pain of living through spiritual principles. We are very fortunate to have had this program. Before, very few people recognized that our gangsters' mentality was an illness. Recovery was only a dream. The responsible, productive, crime free life of successful members, illustrate the effectiveness of our program. Recovery is a reality for us today. By working the steps, we are rebuilding our fractured personalities. Gangsters Anonymous is a healthy environment for growth. As a fellowship, we love and cherish one another, supporting our new way of life together. As we grow, we come to understand humility as acceptance of both our assets and our liabilities. What we want most is to feel good about ourselves. Today, we have real feelings of love, joy, hope, sadness, excitement.

Our feelings are not our old gangster-induced feelings. Sometimes we find ourselves caught up in old ideas, even with time in the program. The basics are always important to recovery. We need to avoid old thinking patterns, both the old ideas and the tendency toward complacency. We cannot afford to become complacent, because our illness is with us twenty-four hours a day. If, while practicing these principles, we allow ourselves to feel superior or inferior, we isolate ourselves. We are headed for trouble if we feel apart from other gangsters. Separation from the atmosphere of recovery and from the spirit of service to others slows our spiritual growth. Complacency keeps us from good will, love and compassion. If we are unwilling to listen to others, we will deny the need for improvement. We learn to become flexible and to admit when others are right and we are wrong. As new things are revealed, we feel renewed. We need to stay open-minded and willing to do that one extra thing, go to one extra meeting, stay on the phone one extra minute, and help a newcomer stay crime free one extra day. This extra effort is vital to our recovery.

We come to know ourselves for the first time. We experience new sensations: to love, to be loved, to know that people care about us and to have concern and compassion for others. We find ourselves doing and enjoying things that we never thought we would be doing. We make mistakes, and we accept and learn from them. We experience failure, and we learn how to succeed. Often we have to face some type of crisis during our recovery, such as the death of a loved one, financial difficulties or divorce. These are realities of life, and they don't go away just because we get crime free. Some of us, even after years of recovery, found ourselves jobless, homeless or penniless. We entertained the thought that staying crime free was not paying off, and the old thinking stirred up self-pity, resentment and anger. No matter how painful life's tragedies can be for us, one thing is clear, we STAY crime free, no matter what!

This is a program of total abstinence. There are times, however, such as in cases of health problems involving surgery and/or extreme physical injury, when medication may be valid. This does not constitute a license to commit crimes, become aggressive and uncaring. There is no safe use of a gangsters' mentality for recovering gangsters. Our minds can't understand the difference between the mentality resulting from pain or our gangster mentality prescribed by ourselves to get by. As gangsters, our skill at self-deception will be at its peak in such situations. Often our minds will manufacture additional pain as an excuse to return to the more comfortable thinking which, for us, is gangster. Turning it over to our Higher Power and getting the support of our sponsor and other members can prevent us from becoming our own worst enemies. Being alone during such times would give our gangster mentality an opportunity to take over. Honest sharing can dispel our fears of old behavior.

Serious illness or surgery can present particular problems for us. Physicians should have specific knowledge of our prior gangster lifestyles. Remember that we, not our doctors, are ultimately responsible for our recovery and our decisions. To minimize the danger, there are a few specific options that we may consider. We use local therapists, avoid our anxiety and anger, become patient while we are still hurting, and spend extra days in (marathon fellowship) in case major issues arise. These are some of our options. Whatever anger or pain we experience will pass. Through prayer, meditation and sharing, we keep our minds off our discomfort and have the strength to keep our priorities in order. It is imperative to keep G.A. members close to us at all times, if possible. It is amazing how our minds will go back to our old gangster-ways and old gangster mentality. You'd be surprised how much pain we can handle without reaching back to our gangster mentality. In this program of total abstinence, however, we need to feel no guilt after having to reach back into our old survival ways in order to protect ourselves or our families.

We often find those who would try to divert us from our new way of living. We must remember what it was like and what it is like now. One bad day crime free is better than our best day living life gangster. In that we know there is no chance of prison or no guilt from the abuse of others. We refuse to allow anyone the opportunity to take our free-time away. A minimum amount of medication may be prescribed by a licensed and informed professional for extreme psychological disorder and subsequent heartache and pain that would ordinarily lead to anger then manifested through violence. We grow through pain in recovery and often find that such a crisis is a gift, an opportunity to experience growth by living crime free.

Before recovery, we were unable to even conceive of the thought that problems brought gifts. This gift may be finding strength within ourselves or regaining the feeling of self-respect that we had lost. Spiritual growth, love, and compassion are idle goals until shared with a fellow gangster. By giving unconditional love in the fellowship, we become more loving, and by sharing spiritual growth we become more spiritual.

By carrying this message to another gangster, we are reminded of our own beginnings. Having had an opportunity to remember old feelings and behaviors, we are able to see our own personal and spiritual growth. In the process of answering the questions of another, our own thinking becomes clearer. Newer members are a constant source of hope, ever reminding us that the program works. We have the opportunity to live the knowledge acquired by staying crime free, when we work with newcomers.

We have learned to value the respect of others. We are pleased when people depend on us. For the first time in our life, we may be asked to serve in positions of responsibility in community organizations outside of G.A. Our opinions are sought and valued by non-gangsters in areas other than gangs and recovery. We can enjoy our families in a new way and may become a credit to them instead of an embarrassment or a burden. They can be proud of us today. Our individual interests can broaden to include social or even political issues. Hobbies and recreation give us new pleasure. It gives us good feelings to know that aside from our value to others as recovering gangsters, we are also of value as human beings. The reinforcement received by sponsorship is limitless. We spent years taking from others in every conceivable way. Words cannot describe the sense of spiritual awareness that we receive when we have given something, no matter how small, to another person. We are each other's eyes and ears. When we do something wrong, our crime free fellowship helps us by showing us what we cannot see.

We sometimes find ourselves caught up in old ideas. We need to constantly review our feelings and thoughts if we are to stay enthusiastic and grow spiritually. This enthusiasm will aid our ongoing recovery. Today we have the freedom of choice. As we work the program to the best of our ability, the obsession with self is removed. Much of our loneliness and fear is replaced by the support and security of the fellowship. Helping a suffering gangster is one of the greatest experiences life has to offer. We are willing to help. We have had similar experiences and understand gangsters as no one else can. We offer hope, for we know that a better way of life is now real for us and we give love because it was given so freely to us. New frontiers are open to us as we learn how to love. Love can be the flow of life energy from one person to another. By caring, sharing, and praying for others, we become a part of them. Through empathy, we allow gangsters to become part of us. As we do this, we undergo a vital spiritual experience and are changed. On a practical level, changes occur because what's appropriate to one phase of recovery may not be for another. We constantly let go of what has served its purpose, and let God guide us through the current phase with what works in the here and now. As we become more God-reliant and qain more self-respect, we realize that we don't need to feel superior or inferior to anyone. Our real value is in being ourselves. Our egos, once so large and dominant, now take a back seat because we are in harmony with a loving God. We find that we lead richer, happier and much fuller life when we lose self-will.

We become able to make wise and loving decisions, based on principles and ideals that have real value in our life. By shaping our thoughts with spiritual ideals, we are freed to become who we want to be. What we had feared, we can now overcome through our dependence on a loving God. Faith has replaced our fear and given us freedom from ourselves. In recovery, we also strive for gratitude. We feel grateful for ongoing God-consciousness. Whenever we confront a difficulty that we do not think we can handle, we ask God to do for us what we cannot do for ourselves. A spiritual awakening is an ongoing process. We experience a wider view of reality as we grow spiritually. An opening of our minds to new spiritual and physical experiences is the key to better awareness. As we grow spiritually, we become attuned to our feelings and our purpose in life.

By loving ourselves, we become able to truly love others. This is a spiritual awakening that comes as a result of living this program. We find ourselves daring to care and love! Higher mental and emotional functions, such as conscience and the ability to love, were sharply affected by our gangster mentality. Living skills were reduced to the animal level. Our spirit was broken. The capacity to feel human was lost. This seems extreme, but many of us have been in this state. In time, through recovery, our dreams came true. We don't mean that we necessarily become rich or famous. However, by realizing the will of our Higher Power, dreams do come true in recovery. One of the continuing miracles of recovery is becoming a productive, responsible member of society. We need to tread carefully into areas that expose us to ego-inflating experiences, or toward prestige and manipulation that may be difficult for us. We have found that the way to remain a productive, responsible member of society is to put our recovery first. G.A. can survive without us, but we cannot survive without G.A. Gangsters Anonymous offers only one promise and that is freedom from active gangster-life, the solution that eluded us for so long. We will be freed from our self-made prisons.

When living just for today, we have no way of knowing what will happen to us. We are often amazed at how things work out for us. We are recovering in the here and now and the future becomes an exciting journey. If we had written down our list of expectations when we came to the program, we would have been cheating ourselves. Hopeless living and hopeless problems have become joyously changed. Our illness has been arrested, and now anything is possible.

We become increasingly open-minded and open to new ideas in all areas of our life. Through active listening, we hear things that work for us. This ability to listen is a gift and grows as we grow spiritually. Life takes on a new meaning when we open ourselves to this gift. In order to receive, we must be willing to give. In recovery, our ideas of fun change. We are now free to enjoy the simple things in life, like fellowship and living in harmony with nature. We now have become free to develop a new understanding of life. As we look back, we are grateful for our new life. It is so unlike the events that brought us here. While living life gangster, we thought that we had fun and that non-gangsters were deprived of it. Spirituality enables us to live life to its fullest, feeling grateful for who we are and for what we have done in life. Since the beginning of our recovery, we have found that joy doesn't come from material things, but from within ourselves. We find that when we lose self-obsession, we are able to understand what it means to be happy, joyous, and free. Indescribable joy comes from sharing from the heart and we no longer need to lie to gain acceptance. Gangsters Anonymous offers gangsters a program of recovery that is more than just a life without crime. Not only is this way of life better than the hell we lived, it is better than any life that we have ever known. We have found a way out, and we see it work for others. Each day tells and shows us this.

Many have tried to understand and explain what it is that creates the gangster. We at Gangsters Anonymous know what creates the individual desire to live life gangster and it is of no real importance. We have heard of everything from lack of a male role model; to ex-cons as parents; to the need to feel a part of something. We have also heard of the most incredible injustice regarding these kids and adults, and that is they are a majority of victims of physical, mental, and sexual child abuse. We at G.A. believe these abuses are too enormous in society in general to aim them so easily at just the gangster. We chose to focus on the thinking involved with this illness, not the cause, which can be so widespread. Of course, walking through walls would be fun; the idea is appealing. However, if you are consumed with the notion of having superhuman powers, something else is probably at work. The explanation is as follows:

We don't feel able to compete on an equal footing with others. We imagine having special abilities that would give us an edge. This response mechanism is generated by feelings of inadequacy. A feeling most of us fight off at some point in our life. So remember, we are not strange or weird for feeling this way. We wish for special powers that would compensate for our real or perceived inadequacies powers that would make us feel more in control of our life and our circumstances where we feel powerless in our everyday life. So we enjoy fantasies where we command the respect and attention of others. We don't feel very effective in our life. We believe things happen to us rather than being able to make things happen. In more extreme instances, being part of the crowd compromises our uniqueness.

If we are "one of them" then we are not special. This causes us to isolate ourselves from others, and we end up retreating to a world of fantasies where we can be and do anything we wish. We should give our goals an overhaul. When was the last time we did this? The fact that we feel powerless or inadequate today may have something to do with expectations we set up either consciously or unconsciously way back to the dinosaur era. But we are not fossils, so why not bring ourselves up to date starting now? Take several minutes to review all our goals and objectives, both short and long term for each of the major areas of our life. Which ones still serve us, and which should go the way of the dinosaur? Get rid of them. All they've been doing is cluttering up our life and making us feel inadequate. Now, based on who we are today and our up to the minute desires, interests, skills, experience base, and levels of motivation, come up with new goals to guide us in the coming months and years.

Remember, successful people don't focus on what they can't do they focus on what they can accomplish. Helen Keller didn't bemoan the fact that she was deaf, mute, and blind; she worked with what she had and inspired millions in the process. We must be clear on exactly what we bring to the table professionally, emotionally, and so on – bring our goals into alignment with this honest self–assessment. There is considerable satisfaction and joy in most goals and dreams; we need only turn our attention to what we can do then do it.

Scenario: We are at a social gathering and all we can think about is what would happen if we walked over to someone and called him every ugly name in the book. We think about jumping up on the table and bursting into song. We mull over the consequences of throwing our glass of wine over the balcony or pulling an all too obvious toupee' off the head of a nearby gentleman. Many people have thoughts like these, and they are, for the most part, fairly harmless. We imagine these scenarios as a mental release. Sometimes the pressures of our life and the continuing social and cultural norms can be restraining. Thoughts of going over the edge and acting thoroughly inappropriate provide a harmless outlet. Sometimes these thoughts are indicative of something more. Put simply, we do not trust ourselves.

We question our judgment and have an underlying fear of doing the very thing that we think about doing. This lack of self-trust manifests into a fear that we may lose control of our rational thought processes and act totally inappropriate. We wonder what would happen if we fell down a flight of stairs or jumped out of a two-story window in the event that we "forgot" that it would not be such a good idea. Part of the creation of these scenarios is planning how we should react after we've done the thinkable. We run through different options that would offer us the least consequence should we lose control of our senses and good judgment.

Do a trust-building exercise with a friend. We are people who know full well how to behave around others. We need to bolster our faith in ourselves and have our trustworthiness reinforced by someone else. A well-known exercise involves being blindfolded and led around by a partner, then reversing the process. We quickly learn to depend on each other and to communicate more effectively, both verbally and non-verbally. Besides, it's a great way to strengthen our bond with someone who's already a friend. Try it and see how it works. In general, any process that calls for teammates to cooperate is an excellent way of building trust. We learn not only to place our trust in others but to live up to the trust they place in us as well. Find a sport that is enjoyable and non-threatening yet offers some measure of healthy competition, such as tennis, badminton, bowling, golfing, racquetball, or horseshoes. Or, indulge in more solitary pursuits that we can still enjoy with a friend, such as nature hiking, mountain bike riding, snorkeling, and so on.

Find a healthy outlet for releasing unsociable urges. Everyone has to let off stream now and then. As we may already have realized, physical activity is one of the best ways of doing this. It's much better to release our aggression in a spirited racquetball match, round of kickboxing, or game of tackle football than it is ways where someone gets hurt. We find ourselves getting upset and liking it. When we're angry, we don't always want to calm down. We hold on to a feeling of anger long after the actual cause of the anger has passed. We feel powerful, more alive, and in control when we're angry. We get angry for many reasons. Feeling hurt, guilty, insecure, powerless or betrayed are just a few of the underlying causes for anger. While anger may be a natural and healthy response to a given situation, holding on to that anger is not. It can lead to a host of psychological and physical ailments not the least of which is depression.

There are several reasons why we hold on to anger. Anger is a powerful emotion and serves as a mask for other feelings, feelings that we would rather not examine and acknowledge. Anyone or a combination of them can be explanations for this response. Thoughts such as inferiority or depression are less likely to surface when we are angry. There may be an emotional void. Anger allows us to feel something, to feel alive. Anger may be the only emotion we can feel that is manifested and maintained to fill this void. Anger may offer us a sense of identity. We need to have something to believe in, something to stand up for. Anger gives us something to feel and generates a passion for something. We may believe that we need anger to give us the impetus to take action and make changes in our life. We need to hit rock bottom before we could turn thing around. We want to generate enough pain in order to motivate ourselves to make a change in our life. It is the only way we feel people will listen to us or respect us. If we do not get angry, others may think that we do not really care enough or are not serious.

Examine whether our anger masks other feelings. When we get angry, what incidents or situations trigger it? We need to identify precisely what we are feeling just before anger kicks in. Does the anger push feelings of hurt, inadequacy, guilt or fear out of the way? These are the feelings that we have not been able to face and they are the reason why we develop anger as a defense mechanism with which to distract ourselves. Anger finds its roots in fear. It is impossible to be angry without first being afraid. We need to investigate the source of our fear. Look at it and examine it objectively. Awareness is a powerful weapon. Do not run away from negative feelings anymore; face them honestly so we can begin to deal with them. Face the anger, know that while it has helped us cope in the past, it does not serve us any longer. Once we understand the reason for anger, it loses its grip on us.

Find excitement in other ways. We may think it is highly impressive to hit rock bottom, then make a dramatic last minute save that completely turns the situation around. Think again. Some of us have been arrested time after time after years of letting ourselves, get fed up, by occasional explosions in which we finally do something. In other words, undergoing pain that could easily have been avoided, we have taught ourselves that life is nothing but a series of life and death crisis. Do we really want to continue living this way? If we can see that the tires on our auto need air, why not handle it now? Why wait until the blowout in the middle of our three hundred mile road trip, go into hysterics, and generally make everyone miserable? If high drama, excitement is what we really crave, there are much better ways to experience it such as skydiving, hang-gliding, rock–climbing, racecar driving, and speedboat racing. There are any number of thrill sports and adventure excursions that allow us to really test our metal. Go for it! Live!

We need to experiment with different expressions of

power and broaden our leadership skills. Passion, strength, and conviction are admirable qualities, indeed. E need to learn to channel the fire and intensity of our anger intelligently so that people respect us and do not fear us. Harsh, blistering words and behaviors are not the only way to get people to listen. In fact, everyone knows that bullies are cowards at heart. We stray away from bullying by showing that we are in control of our actions and cognizant of their effects. Few things command respect more instantly than quiet, carefully modulated words surrounding an edge of steel.

Identify with strength, passion, and courage, not with anger. Learn the difference between aggressiveness and assertiveness. The use of leadership books, tape programs, seminars, and other courses invest in our education. Learn what has made world leaders so great and study the qualities of the people in Gangsters Anonymous whom we admire the most. STEP UP!

One of Many True Stories to come.

From Gang Banging to Culture Banging

I'm a 35 year old Black man from the great city of Los

Angeles; born and raised in the inner city in a place called, "The Low Bottom Projects". Mama was a part of the Black Movement and a gangster girl. My daddy was a dope fiend, bank robber and a member of a prison based group called the B.G.F. He was never really a part of my life. Financially I was provided for with the best of clothes, toys, bikes, trips to the zoo, and Magic Mountain. My grandfather, "Sport"; played for the Negro Baseball League, took me to Lakers basketball games, Dodgers games etc. He showed me how to play baseball, box, basketball, and listen to music. Music was a big part of the family; jazz, blues, gospel, soul, and funk. I went to Black Panther Rallies, the Watts Festivals, church and Islamic Temples. On the other hand, mama was heavy into drugs, checks, and the Ho game, therefore she had me hold stuff, count money and stay all night with street girls. I would make drop offs at an early age, saw people killed, pimps, hoes etc. I was also an abused child, beat up, and beat up by my mom's uncle. It was just my brother and me at the time and we were close.

My life flipped when moms went to prison and the child services took my brother to a foster home and put me in a placement home, by which time I had already joined a gang. After that, I went to live with my grandparents in my neighborhood, my daddies uncles were BLOODS so they took me in real close. My first act of violence at age twelve was to show my uncle that I was a gangster, was robbery. Then came dope dealing and then hard-core banging. At that time I was drinking, smoking Sherm. I went to three High schools. While at Morningside High school, I met my future wife. She got pregnant and that to me was really cool, a little me. I still did crimes but this time it was for my girl and baby. I've been shot three times. The worst case was in the year 1989 when I was shot in the leg with an AK-47 automatic assault rifle while trying to rob a gambling shack. I went to prison for a shooting and while inside I sold drugs, gangbanged and played politics etc. The only thing I cared about was getting buffed, long hair and Tattoos. When I was released, it was the same old BS the wife and me started a business pushing dope out of town. The money was good, we were ghetto rich.

My wife and I broke up because I was cheating. I started drinking again and smoking on a daily basis. Now my mama was on crack and lived from spot to spot. My brother was in jail. My sister was placed in a foster home. I failed to mention she was born in prison. Then the 92 riot changed my life. I was part of the "Peace" between the Bloods and Crips. I started learning about my people and our history. I started meeting black folks like Maxine Waters, Jim Brown, Rosa Parks, Angela Davis, and Louis Farrakhan. I became racist toward white people and I reunited with my wife. We had a second child and I was then working with Jim brown talking to the youth during Black Events. I sold Tee Shirts, cassettes tapes, soda, etc. I enrolled in South West College while I was collecting GR. I stopped committing crimes, using drugs and became a family man, until my money started getting funny. I went back to the hood and started slanging. This became a big problem with my relationship soon I eventually went back to jail and joined a Black Militant Organization. I started snorting cocaine in 1996.I was taking girls on profiles, busting checks, hanging out in Hollywood a lot, living the club life. In 1991 I really started looking at my life and having flashbacks about my childhood, being shot, beat-up by the police, fights etc. Therefore, I started taking psyche medication for stress, depression, violence, etc. I am in the biggest fight of my life; the fight with the enemy within. Still I like the power, money, hookers. The bottom line, I begin realizing that I needed help. Thank You Gangsters Anonymous for opening your doors for people like me. I need to change my ways so I can see my kids grow-up and give back to my community. T.

Kenny G's Story

As a kid, I was very aggressive and mean spirited. I can only say I mimicked the only personality that was in my home. I grew to have a fondness for guns at an early age. My brother and I would hunt birds with a pump pellet BB gun. He and I were both good shots. We moved to Los Angeles in the early 70's. I remember the day we flew in and drove passed a gas station where we saw a large group of men on motorcycles. My older brother asked what and who they were. My Aunt answered and told us all they were the Hell's Angels. A motorcycle gang. They were known to be a tough bunch of people that did not take any junk. My older brother commented that he wanted to be a member of a motorcycle gang because he was just as tough.

After living in L.A. for a few months, we began to see the difference in how the kids treated each other. I knew then I had a problem making friends but I did not know how bad it was until I started school. I began fighting and getting beat up. I met up with a kid that was known as the school king and nobody fooled around with him. We became good friends because I would make him laugh. I was the class clown and could talk about anyone with great skill. I still fought but I was not scared of retaliation any more because of my new Homey.

My gang life began when another friend and I met Big Mike. BM began to teach us how to flip and to walk and talk like gangsters. We noticed this style very easy because we both considered ourselves rough any way. That was one of the reasons BM approached us. He said he liked the way we carried ourselves. Meatball and I began traveling around town competing with any one capable of doing somersaults. (Flips). No one could beat MB because he could do more flips and quicker with full backs back to back to back-to-back. Unfortunately, I could not flip a pancake. We never fought but flipped all over town.

After one particular fight, a person that everyone was afraid of chased me home. My mother heard about me running home from school and decided to take me out. She enrolled me into a private school. I never fit in this school, because everyone there had a mom, a dad, and a home and had dinner around the dining table. I fought there and was beaten up a few times. I was then asked to leave. I then checked into a public Junior High. I graduated from there after being picked on and fighting back. When I arrived in High School, I was introduced to all of the gangbangers in my grade. I was soon to find out that my older brother was one of the toughest gangbangers there. I began my gangster life in full force in the ninth grade. I took on the title and stood my post. I fought and played the gun game and many people fought and shot at me. Luckily, I survived the wars. After graduating High School, I began to use drugs and party most every night. Bar fights and prison bars became my past time. I began to notice my criminal life was beginning to close in on me. I tried quitting the clubbing and drinking scene many times with no results. My last altercation was with a teenager. I lost the fight and decided this was it. I am tired of the hospitals and jails. I am tired of never knowing the outcome of my next adventure. I wanted to live. Thanks to Gangsters Anonymous, I now have a life. I am not the best I can be. I am still growing, I am glad I am who I am today and the lifestyle I live today is much better than my best day as a gangster. G.A. has given me a life to be grateful of.

Your story is needed to continue supporting the still suffering gangster. Send all stories: 2245 E Colorado Blvd. Suite 104-112 Pasadena, CA 91107

No major crime details please. Keep it simple.

WORDS TO REMIND US OF OUR WALK... A day at a time

Alcoholics Anonymous Original Steps and Traditions

THE TWELVE STEPS

1. We admitted we were powerless over alcohol – that our life had become unmanageable.

2. Came to believe that a power greater than ourselves could restore us to sanity.

3. Made a decision to turn our will and our life over to the care of God as we understood Him.

4. Made a searching and fearless moral inventory of ourselves.

5. Admitted to God, to ourselves, and to another human being the exact nature of our wrongs.

6. Were entirely ready to have God remove all these defects of character.

7. Humbly asked Him to remove our shortcomings.

8. Made a list of all persons we had harmed, and became willing to make amends to them all.

9. Made direct amends to such people wherever

possible, except when to do so would injure them or others.

10. Continued to take personal inventory and when we were wrong, promptlym admitted it.

11. Sought though prayer and meditation to improve our conscious contact with God as we understood Him, praying only for knowledge of His will for us and the power to carry that out.

12. Having had a spiritual awakening as the result of these steps, we tried to carry this message to alcoholics and to practice these principles in all our affairs.

–Reprinted with permission of A.A. World Services, Inc.

THE TWELVE TRADITIONS

1. Our common welfare should come first; personal recovery depends upon A.A. unity.

2. For our group purpose there is but one ultimate authority – a loving God as He may express Himself in our group conscience. Our leaders are but trusted servants; they do not govern.

3. The only requirement for A.A. membership is a

desire to stop drinking.

4. Each group should be autonomous except in matters affecting other groups or A.A. as a whole.

5. Each group has but one primary purpose – to carry its message to the alcoholic who still suffers.

6. An A.A. group ought never endorse, finance or lend the A.A. name to any related facility or outside enterprise, lest problems of money, property and prestige divert us from our primary purpose.

7. Every A.A. group ought to be fully self-supporting, declining outside contributions.

8. Alcoholics Anonymous should remain forever non-professional, but our service centers may employ special workers.

9. A.A., as such, ought never be organized; but we may create service boards or committees directly responsible to those they serve.

10. Alcoholics Anonymous has no opinion on outside issues; hence the A.A. name ought never be drawn into public controversy.

11. Our public relations policy is based on attraction rather than promotion; we need always maintain personal anonymity at the level of press, radio and films.

12. Anonymity is the spiritual foundation of all our

traditions, ever reminding us to place principles before personalities.

CPSIA information can be obtained
at www.ICGtesting.com
Printed in the USA
FSHW02n2034260818
51780FS